Create Your Personal
POWER PLAN
For a Healthy, Happy, Fulfilling Life

by Alice C. Potter

Illustrated by Elena Facciola

Cover illustration
by Chris "Honeysuckle" Ellis

Cover by Brian Groppe

RONIN
Berkeley, CA.

Create Your Personal
POWER PLAN
For a Healthy, Happy, Fulfilling Life

by Alice C. Potter

Illustrated by Elena Facciola

Cover illustration
by Chris "Honeysuckle" Ellis

Cover by Brian Groppe

RONIN
Berkeley, CA

Create Your Personal Power Plan
For a Healthy, Happy, Fulfilling Life

Copyright 2019 by Estate of Alice C Potter

ISBN: 9781579512750 Pbook
ISBN: 9781579512767 Ebook

Published by
Ronin Publishing, Inc.
PO Box 3436
Oakland, CA 94609
www.roninpub.com

Production:

Manuscript derrivation: Beverly A. Potter.

Cover Design: Brian Groppe.

Book Design: Beverly A. Potter.

Cover illustration: Chris "Honeysuckle" Ellis

Illustrations by Elena Facciola

Library of Congress Card Number: 2019931622

Distributed to the book trade by PGW/Ingram.

Derived from *The Positive Thinker,* 978-0425142578, 240 pg., Berkley Books, Mass Market, 1994.

Acclaim for Alice C. Potter's
Personal Power Plan

". . . more than a feel-good book—it's a road map that can help anyone, no matter where they start, to have a more successful and rewarding, fulfilling life. Read it to enoy it, follow its advice and the sky is the limit."

—Patricia Fripp
President National Speakers Assoc
author of *Get What You Want*

" . . . a gold mine of practical ideas to help you change negative patterns. SPecifically, it will help you change the harmful chatter in you head to produce dislogue that will help you readh higher toward your goals."

—Daniel G. Amen, M.D.
author of *Don't Shoot Yourself in the Foot*

"Down-to-earth practical suggesiton for getting started on your Personal Power Program!"

—*Ruth Ross*
author of *Prospering Woman and Power to Prosper*

" . . . provides an insightful, comprehensive blueprint for all to create a rewarding life."

—Susan Scott
author of *Create the Love of Your LIfe*

Table of Contents

Other Books by Alice C. Potter

The Positive Thinker
Self-Motivating Strategies for Personal Success
Create Your Personal Power Plan
is a derrivative of The Positive Thinker.

I Can Do That!

Putting the Positive Thinker to Work

The Positive Thinker's 10 Commandments

Preface

Create Your Perosnal Power Plan offers a proven formula for happiness and success in manifesting personal desires. It guides you in looking at where you are right now—your present state of mind and affairs. You will explore the past personal programming that made you into the unique individual you are today. You will analyze your thinking, attitudes, and conversations with yourself and how they contribute to or hinder your health, happiness, and success in each area of your life.

Age-old universal laws and how they affect your life are discussed. The universal laws are irrefutable, constant, and impartial; they apply to everyone, everywhere, and at all times. A proper understanding of these powerful invisible forces is essential for you to achieve optimum results from the new positive thinking skills you will learn.

You will learn how to prepare yourself for the most important personal project you will ever undertake in this lifetime. You will learn to lay the groundwork for the preparation of your personal programming and reprogramming through your Personal Power Plan.

The Personal Power Plan, or PPP, is a *personal* plan because you write it and you record it. It is a *power* plan because it works with powerful invisible forces. It will produce the future you desire when you follow the plan. The three steps of the plan are as follows: First, determine exactly what you want in your life in every category and down to the smallest detail. Second, write your life script to read the way you want your future to be.

Next, record your script utilizing proven methods, including contemporary advertising principles used by the media. The end result becomes your Personal Power Plan, which is as individual as your fingerprints.

Your Personal Power Plan will guide your actions. It challenges you to make the most important choice of your life. Make the choice that will assure the future of your dreams. You and you alone have the power to do it, The choice is yours; the time is now!

Introduction

What do you want out of life? What do you want to be when you grow up? What would make you really happy? More money? A better job? Career recognition? A college degree? Feeling self-assured and confident?

Do you want to feel in control of your life? Develop a new relationship? To be a loving wife or husband? Make new friends? Live in the home of your dreams? Drive a Mercedes, Jaguar, or BMW? Wear an elegant wardrobe? Have better health? Have a perfect body? Have kids who behave? Enjoy security in your retirement years? Have serenity and peace of mind? Have a sense of union with a higher power?

We all have desires and aspiraton, but many go unfulfilled because we consider them to be just dreams.

We all have desires and aspirations, but many go unfulfilled. We consider them simply dreams. Many live lives of "quiet desperation." Many consider themselves lucky if when they succeed in one area of life, usually career, because that is where most people focus their greatest attention, at the expense of other areas such as health, family, personal relationships, and spiritual commitment.

What if you could have it all? What if you could write your own life script—and live it? What if you could make your dreams and aspirations come true now—or in not too distant future? Would you be interested? Of course you would!

I've mentioned a lot of "what ifs". But let me tell you—there are no ifs, ands, or buts about this—you can fulfill all of your dreams right now in this lifetime. It's all up to you. *Yes, it's all up to you. You are in charge.* You have the power to create your life exactly the way you want it

We each have unlimited personal power within ourselves.

or to change it to be the way you want it to be. Right now you can take control and begin to live your personal hopes and dreams. Sound incredible? It is true.

Naturally, you're skeptical, but if you're curious, you'll want to know how to accomplish such lofty goals. After all, if it were within everyone's power, wouldn't everyone have everything they want and need and—more importantly, wouldn't everyone be happy? Most people have never honestly asked themselves that all-important question. They didn't realize it was up for consideration. If they did ask, they may never have sincerely searched for the answer. Or, after asking, they never come to the realization that the means to achieve their dreams lies within themselves. For the most part, we are all too often unaware of our personal power.

In the following pages, you will learn about the unlimited personal power within you, how to tap into it, and how to put your personal power to work for you. You will be given age-old laws and truths, basic rules and instructions that have been part of the philosophies of the world's great sages

You will learn how to apply these universal truths to your life here and now.

and leaders. Best of all, you will learn how to apply these universal truths to your life here and now.

1

Mental Chatter
How To Stop it

The human mind is an amazing computer. Well, if it's so great, then why is your mind screwing you up? It's the programming, obviously. Remember the old acronym, GIGO, meaning garbage in—garbage out or garbled in—garbled out? That's pretty self-explanatory, isn't it? If you program your computer improperly or with erroneous material—garbage, that's what you're going to get out—garbage. Very simply, if your mind has been programmed with garbage or garbled material, you cannot expect to retrieve anything from it but garbage or garbled material.

If your mind has been programmed with garbage or garbled material, you cannot expect to retrieve anything from it but garbage or garbled material.

So simple, in fact, that it is profound. Most profound truths are simple, which confuses people. We expect profound to mean difficult, mysterious, or hard-to-understand. The GIGO concept is simplicity itself; basic, down-to-earth, factual and, when understood, easy to implement. Basic truth: our minds are programmed and that is why we think, act, and feel the way we do, We program ourselves—self-program—daily, every day, during all of our waking moments, as well as when sleeping since our minds are active in dreaming.

We Are Programmed

If we are all programmable, why don't we just program ourselves the way we want to be, the way we dream of being? Why do we simply accept ourselves the way we are? Most of us have not given this much thought, even though we're thinking all the time. If you don't believe it, just try not thinking for a minute. Go ahead: STOP THINKING NOW! Do not think about anything for just one minute.

What happened? You couldn't stop your thoughts, right? We couldn't turn off your mind, with the constant thoughts, the inner dialogue— the incessant chatter that psychologists call "self-talk". We are all the same in this regard. Our minds are filled with endless, largely uncontrolled thoughts. Is this self-talk productive? How

do you like what you're saying to yourself? Does your self-talk make you happy?

Are your thoughts getting you where you want to go? If you're like most people, the thoughts seem to be "just there". Similar thoughts have always been there, so you accept them.

If thoughts weren't in your mind, what would be there? A vacuum? Nothing? How can you think nothing? You just tried and you were unable to stop thinking!

Everyone has spontaneous thoughts. Why be concerned with these random thoughts? They are basically mundane, uneventful, or at least not evil. You've made it to adulthood—maturity—maybe even middle age. What's the problem?

Computers are "programmed" with a programming language like Java, FORTRAN, or Pascal, as examples. A programming language is a vocabulary and set of grammatical rules for instructing a computing device to perform specific tasks. You may have a "rule" in your thinking that says "I get depressed when ignored", whereas another person may have a thinking rule that says "I act to get attention when ignored".

Rewrite Programs to Change Your Life

If you rewrite your programming—rewrite your scripts—you will change your actions and reactions and thereby change your life, your physical and mental health, your quality of life, find peace of mind, and achieve your goals. 'That's a big order, but that's precisely why it's so exciting. There's no need to stop with the achievements just mentioned. You can do all of these things and everything else you truly desire. Results are

unique. You are in charge. You become the pup-
pet master. You and you alone are in charge of
your self-program—your individual program
conceived by you and for you and no one but
you! You can write your own program just the
way you want it.

Since our mind can be likened to a computer, and we agree that we've all been programmed, it follows that our life is a kind of printout. That is so important that I must say

Do you know why you think the way you do?

it again. Our life is a printout. Our emotions, our feelings, our health, our happiness, our successes and failures, our futures are printouts from our personal computers. To change our personal printout, we must first look at our random thoughts and analyze them.

Listen to them, if that's more appropriate. Not being inside your mind, I can't really imagine what's going on there. I only know what people tell me goes on in their minds and what goes on in mine. If you could tap into my mind, this is what you would find: words, sentences, paragraphs, chapters, vignettes, novellas, short stories, proposed phone calls, explanations, excuses, rationalizations, and more, all carefully constructed, usually grammatically correct dissertations, and always in English, of course. People who are multilingual sometimes say they don't know which language they think in.

Maybe they think in pictures or feelings. But I can hardly think that words do not play a very important part. Regardless of how you think—in words, pictures, or feelings—The Personal Power Plan will work for you because you know how you think and can adapt the program to fit the unique you.

Although you may know how you think, do you know why you think the way you do? More than likely both the how's and why's date back to your infancy and the big programmers in your life—your parents. Parents are usually well-meaning people, but they are human and fallible. So you were initially programmed by a couple of amateurs who were acting out their own faulty programming, learned from a previous set of big programmers—their parents.

My friend Hans was born in East Germany.
During the war, his family was forced out of
their home with the clothes on their backs and
what they could carry. His father spent time as a
prisoner of war. Later, his family was fortunate
to find a sponsor in this country, which enabled
them to immigrate to the United States. Here,
his father worked as a barber, his mother was a
domestic and took care of children. They both
worked hard and put in long hours.

In school, Hans's classmates laughed at his
accent and ridiculed his clothing. Hans worked
at odd jobs before and after school, delivering
papers, polishing shoes, bagging groceries—any-

thing that would help his parents financially and allow him to buy more appropriate clothes. Hans's family never bought a home; they always rented. His parents believed home ownership was for the wealthy and privileged, not for the working class. It's safer to rent than to take on a big mortgage, they reminded Hans whenever the subject came up. His father had several opportunities to open his own shop but never did so; being in business for oneself was risky, he repeatedly told his wife and son; it's better and safer to be an employee than an employer. No one in Hans's family had ever attended college.

College was for the upper class, above their station in life, they told Hans again and again. Hans was programmed for mediocrity by his parents. His parents meant well. They sincerely wanted to protect themselves and their son from the financial risks and possible pitfalls of home ownership, business entrepreneurship, and academic competition. They were acting out the programming they had learned from their parents and previous generations brought up under the old European system of class consciousness. Nevertheless, against the advice of his parents, Hans attended college and received his degree in computer science.

Hans was able to break the chain of ongoing parental programming. How? He tells me that people in this country think differently. The idea of equal opportunity really rang a bell for him. He observed people from a variety of backgrounds and all walks of life succeeding here based on their individual efforts and ambition. His parents came from, or thought they came from, a particular station in life, but Hans realized he did not have to be stuck with their concepts. Hans accepted personal responsibility for his future and he worked to break an ongoing pattern to make sure that his future would be the success that he knew he could make it be.

Who Are the Programmers?

Big programmers are primary, but they are just the beginning. Next in line are the assistant advisors: aunts and uncles, nieces and nephews, brothers and sisters not to mention neighbors and friends and, as you advance in years, schoolmates and coworkers. Among other areas of influence, assistant advisors contribute to sibling rivalry—that very influential programming known as peer pressure—and what is known as keeping up with the Joneses.

I live in Oakland, California. It is a beautiful city with a bad reputation. Daily, to my dismay, I read about dire rising crime rate in Oakland. An increasing number of our cities' young

The authorities can have a very beneficial influence on you or an extremely disastrous one.

people are bending to the pressure of their peers. The result is the increased use of drugs and firearms by those who seem to feel that these will solve their problems. Some assistant advisors carry a great deal of weight.

Then there are the authorities: teachers, bosses, and political leaders. These people all affect the way you think. The authorities can have a very beneficial influence on you or an extremely disastrous one, depending upon their power and your dependence and vulnerability when under their direction. Good authority figures can inspire, motivate, direct, and lead. Bad or unethical ones can cause irreparable damage to those who come under their command and who must bow to their power.

Many people have a favorite teacher story. Recently, at a meeting of the National Speakers Association, George R. Walther, a dynamite speaker and author of *Power Talking: 50 Ways to Say What You Mean and Get What You Want*, told the story of the impact one of his early teachers had on his life. George's father, Merle, had the potential to be a big-league baseball player. The big programmer in Merle's life, his father, decided the high rolling life of baseball was not for Merle; he would go to college and study electronics instead. Merle was heartbroken, but there was no arguing with his father. Years later, when George was born, what do you suppose Merle wanted for his son? To play baseball, of course, baseball and team sports did not interest George; he avoided them. Instead, he excelled in Junior Achievement, sales, and academic programs.

Later, he majored in Rhetoric and Public Address. George received no support from his father, but one of his authorities, his eighth-grade teacher, Madaien Rentz, from Central School in San Carlos, California, encouraged him in his speaking endeavors.

When George Walther spoke to the Northern California Chapter of the National Speakers Association, he produced a letter from Mrs. Rentz written to him in 1963 that he'd saved over the years. The letter said, in part, "Yesterday's speech was the highlight. There could have been no doubt in the minds of your listeners about your sincerity, honesty, and integrity... You have gained stature in their respect and admiration of your peers and teachers." Lacking support from his father, George leaned heavily on the encouragement of a very influential authority in his life, his teacher. When I talked to George about the programming he'd received from his teacher, George said, "Yes, Alice, Mrs. Rentz did a good job of programming me. My brochure shows what can happen when you tell someone he speaks well." If she could see and hear him now, Mrs. Rentz would be very, very proud.

Finally, there are the home frontiers: spouses and one's own offspring. If you don't think your kids affect the way you think and act, look around while shopping at the grocery store or mall and notice the number of real-life grown-ups being programmed by their three- to five-year-olds. It's difficult not to be programmed by those close to us in the intimate setting of the home, and this is not necessarily bad. Certainly, input from our loved ones is to be expected, considered, and used when appropriate. But becoming slavishly dependent or subservient to one's spouse, toddler, or teenager is not healthy and is to be discouraged. If you ever watch daytime TV talk shows, you'll find yourself exposed to a large dose of true stories of home frontier programming. Yes, there still are macho men, wife and child abusers, and manipulators of all ages in our midst.

Peripheral Programmers

Don't overlook the peripheral programmers who also took part in shaping your thoughts and probably still do; they have with ideas about gender, racial and economic conditions, nationality, religion, and other relevant circumstances. The peripheral programmers probably become the most powerful programmers of all once you enter the outside world. Ideas perpetuated by them contribute to sexual harassment, race riots like the ones we've seen in L.A. and other major cities, scandals, the ongoing religious wars in such places as Ireland and Israel, and the deeply hurt feelings many experience from thoughtless sexual, racial, religious, and political slurs. Do you remember Jim Jones of Jonestown? Yes, peripheral programmers can be very powerful indeed.

By the touch of a switch, we also continue our own insidious programming with our radios and televisions and the station's or network's chosen programming and commercials. Then there's all the printed matter we're exposed to daily, such as newspapers, books, magazines, flyers, and junk mail. These are our outside influencers. One of the most notorious outside influencers that I remember from my childhood was Orson Welles. Back in the thirties he scared the daylights out of New Jersey residents during the famous broadcast in which he warned that men from Mars were descending upon the steate. Welles influenced many reasonable people to leave their homes and take to the hills!

So far, it appears that most, if not all, of your input has come from sources outside yourself and over which you had little control. During your formative years, this definitely applies; later, you probably did have some choices. As an adult, you supposedly could choose which books, newspapers, and magazines to read and which radio and television programs to listen to or watch. But how careful were you about those choices? Even if great care were taken in your reading or listening material, you were still reading and listening to other people's words and other people's ideas, not your own. We've all heard that most television programs are geared to the intellectual level of a twelve-year-old. Is that who you are?

Domino Effect

Are you getting the picture of the awesome, multiplying effect this amount of programming can have on you as an individual? Is it any wonder we're all so mixed up and in such definite and dire need to gain or regain control of our thoughts and, ultimately, our lives? Because we're programmed by virtually everyone and everything in our lives, it only makes sense that we also contribute to the programming of those with whom we come in contact, often in detrimental ways, without our even realizing it.

Are you getting the picture of the awesome, multiplying effect this amount of programming can have on you as an individual?

You've heard of the domino effect. How often does it take place in your daily routine? Example: In the morning you don't hear the alarm and oversleep. In rushing around to get ready for work, you stub your toe. You want to blame someone, so you yell at your spouse or dog and choke on your morning coffee. You have a near-miss fender bender on the freeway as you snarl at fellow commuters and contribute negatively to their day. By the time you get to work, you've decided the world is against you and you proceed to take it out on the office staff. You ruin your secretary's day with your curt remarks and grouchy mood—who passes that mood along to all the customers she comes in contact with over the phone. Throughout the day, like the falling dominos, it goes on and on. In a very short period of time, you have, perhaps unknowingly, impacted a great many lives.

By regaining and maintaining control of our thoughts and actions, we can contribute positively, rather than negatively, to the happiness and productivity of everyone around us. We are all interrelated so, unless we are isolated on a desert island, it is imperative to know and understand that our actions, attitudes, beliefs, and conduct have a far-reaching ripple effect that can impact everyone around us. Therefore, not only does it make sense, but it's also our right, duty, and responsibility to reprogram ourselves for our own health, happiness, prosperity, and peace of mind in order to help create a harmonious atmosphere for those around us and, ultimately, those around the world.

If you agree that reprogramming is not only reasonable but a great idea, I say, let's do it! Let's reprogram you to be who you want to be, to have what you want to have, and to feel the way you want to feel. That's what this book, and the Personal Power Plan is all about. Let's start now. If you want to change—or if you want things and circumstances in your life to change—if you want them to change dramatically or just to improve slightly, you must start now. Your future is being created now, this day, this hour, this minute, and the sooner you start to change your personal programming with your very own Personal Power Plan, the sooner you will start to create positive changes in every area of your life and realize the incredibly bright and bountiful future that's rightfully yours.

Your first step is to read this book. Then start programming yourself with your own desired material. Choose your own words, your own ideas, your own needs and desires, your own thoughts about success, your own goals, and program them into your mental computer. Instead of garbage in—garbage out, which is what you've teen getting all these years, you'll change your personal GIGO to good in—good out or, better still, great in—great out!

2

Rocks in Your Head

Law Of Substitution

Are you familiar with the term, "You've got rocks in your head"? It means you're crazy, your ideas are all wrong, you're stupid, a klutz, that'll never work. The only way to change that negativity to positivity is to get rights in your head. You must replace the rocks—or wrongs—with rights. Every wrong idea, thought, attitude, or concept presently occupying space in your head must be replaced with a right, or positive, idea, thought, attitude, or concept.

Suppose, for most of your waking day, and probably without being consciously

We constantly talk to ourselves and accept what we say as fact. This is self-programming.

ROCKS IN YER HEAD

aware of it, you say to yourself, "I'm too short—or too fat," or "I'm too young—or too old," or "I'm not qualified—I'm not good enough." These thoughts—this self-talk—may relate to a job, a social situation, or almost any area of life. Maybe your constant internal rant is, "I'll never get it right, I always blow it, I'm just plain stupid." Your belief system, after such constant and ongoing input, will accept these negative observations as total fact and, therefore, you will perform in just that manner because that is precisely how you've programmed yourself to behave.

When you change negative ideas to positive ones by telling yourself, "I am perfect just the way

I am," "I am qualified for the proposed job/situation," or *"I always do the right things at the right times," your belief system, after constant and ongoing input of this positive nature will accept the revision and that's how you will perform.

Theory of Displacement

Because they are opposites and in conflict, both wrongs and rights cannot occupy your mind at the same time. If your head—your mental computer—is filled with right ideas and positive thoughts, there's simply no room for the negative thoughts. Just as it is an absolute scientific fact that two objects cannot occupy the same place at the same time, two different thoughts cannot occupy your mind at the same time. You cannot think positively and negatively simultaneously. You can replace negative thoughts with positive

Pearls of wisdom

negative water

thoughts, one at a time, thereby eventually replacing all of your rocks with rights. This is called "the law of substitution". Your Personal Power Plan, or PPP, which will be explained in great detail in following chapters, is an easy, natural, practical, and proven way to implement the law of substitution.

The law of substitution says replace negative thoughts with positive ones.

The theory of displacement offers another way of looking at this concept. This theory also uses rocks to illustrate the point, but this time the rocks represent positive thoughts, attitudes, and attributes. To avoid confusion, let us call these rocks pearls of wisdom or golden nuggets, imagine a bucket of water—negative water. Each time we drop a pearl or golden nugget into the negative water—which represents the thoughts we hold in our minds—we displace the negativity in direct proportion to the size and weight or strength of the positive pearl or nugget. Drop enough positive pearls and nuggets into your bucket of negative water and watch what happens.

Soon your negative programming will be displaced. It will have flowed over the top of the bucket and simply flowed away. Your bucket will then be full of optimistic, positive thoughts, attitudes, and attributes, while the negativity will have been totally displaced.

If you suffer from low self-esteem, lack of appreciation for your tremendous potential, or are simply going through a period of depression, you will definitely benefit from utilizing the law of substitution and the theory of displacement to oust whatever negativity you've been harboring. One way to start doing this—right now before reading any further—is to compose a list of positive characteristics you wish to possess. State each one in the present tense in a positive manner. Write these statements, which we call "affirmations", on cards or simply memorize them and read or repeat these statements to yourself until they are ingrained in your mind and your subconscious. When you believe what you say to yourself, which will happen in time thanks to the miraculous workings of your subconscious mind, you will act on these affirmations.

You become what you say to yourself.

You become what you say to yourself. You will become what you wish to be. Affirmations and how to write them, an integral part of your Personal Power Plan, will be explained in detail later in this book.

What else can you do in the meantime, before you learn about and begin your Personal Power Plan? What can you do right now to bring that relentless, ongoing tape in your mind under control? What can you do to stamp out negativity and its counterparts, fear and worry? Here are a few suggestions.

Cancel! Stop! Halt!

Pick the "stop" word that feels best to you. I prefer "cancel" because, to me, cancel goes far beyond stop or halt. Webster's defines cancel: "to destroy the force, effectiveness or validity of; to annul; to bring to nothingness; to neutralize."

That's precisely what I want to do with my negative thoughts, so I shout, "Cancel," when they attack. Stop and halt are single-syllable four-letter words, as are most expletives, and you may, therefore, favor one of those. Pick whichever word does it for you. Then, have one or more affirmations, or positive statements, worded to your liking, ready to substitute for the negative thought.

An affirmation is a positive thought or declaration that you state in the present tense as if it were a fact, that you consciously choose to immerse in your subconscious in order to produce a desired result. Or, if you're not ready to get into affirmations just yet, simply replace the negative, disturbing or worry thought with a pleasant, happy thought. In other words, change the subject.

When you hear yourself talking negative to yourself, running on your mental tape or you're in the midst of a negative thinking pattern, say "Cancel!" or "Stop!" or "Halt!" or any other expletive that gets the message across and immediately replace the negative thought with your positive affirmation or pleasant thought.

An affirmation is a positive thought or declaration that you state in the present tense as if it were a fact, that you consciously choose to immerse in your subconscious in order to produce a desired result.

A good healthy out-loud shout can do absolute wonders in impressing your mind with the fact that the negative thought is unacceptable and must be replaced.

For example, suppose you're planning to ask for a raise or promotion and your mental tape is running a number on you stating, "I'll never get that raise. I'm scared. Maybe I can't handle it. I'm stupid. I won't even ask." That kind of thinking will not only not get you the raise or promotion, it may even be counterproductive when you finally go to see the boss. Cancel, stop, or halt that negative thinking! Instead, fill your mind with the many positives you have to offer him and the organization, saying to yourself, I am totally competent in my job. I am an exemplary employee, and I am deserving of a suitable raise or promotion."

If you're in public, you may prefer to say your stop word and affirmation to yourself, but frequently these thoughts come on when we're alone and a good healthy out-loud shout can do absolute wonders in impressing your mind with the fact that the negative thought is unacceptable and must be replaced. If you're not into loud verbalization—shouting, try doing it in the closet with the door shut or shout when in the shower with the water running. Don't compound matters by having the neighbors call the police because they think an attack may be taking place.

This method is one of my favorites and one I use constantly when I find, to my dismay, that I'm harboring negative thoughts of any kind, especially worry thoughts, one of the most treacherous and destructive kinds of negative thinking. Whenever my imagination goes berserk in this particular worry area, I bring in my good old faithfuls: cancel, stop, and halt. Originally, with what I considered big worries, I was a closet cancel-shouter, but now the power of the word cancel, silently spoken, works for me.

The Rubber Band Technique

This is an oldie in psychological circles, but it works. Put an ordinary rubber band on your wrist. Or, if you want to be fancy, you can wear

an elastic pony-tail hair band that's color coordinated with your outfit. When the inevitable negative thought makes itself known, snap the band while saying Stop! Cancel! or Halt! to yourself or out loud. Then replace the negative thought with your positive affirmation.

After a few days of snapping a rubber band, combined with a lot of stop-shouting, plus appropriate replacement thoughts, the pain diminished and I was on my way to being free.

This technique may sound ridiculously simple, but don't discount it. It can work wonders and I can personally attest to its effectiveness. Many years ago, after the breakup of a long-term relationship, I was devastated, or so I thought at the time. I couldn't get the individual out of my mind or concentrate on my work. I was literally making myself miserable through my untamed thoughts. I would dwell on the happy moments of the relationship, conveniently forgetting all the bad times. I thought, "If we'd just try it one more time, everything would be perfect." Of course, that was wishful thinking at its worst.

Every time those fantasy thoughts would run rampant in my mind, I'd snap that rubber band and, out loud if I were alone or, silently if in public, I'd say, "Stop"—vehemently. "Stop thinking about him!" In this situation, stop worked better for me than cancel. Then I would remind myself of all the reasons why the relationship ended and why it had to stay that way. And, more importantly, I would tell myself that if I ever expected to have the kind of loving, mutually respectful relationship that I really wanted, one that would work with a new, more appropriate partner, I had to let go of the past. I had to empty myself of past emotional baggage in order to open myself to someone new.

Believe it or not, after a few days of snapping a rubber band, combined with a lot of stop-shouting, plus appropriate replacement thoughts, the pain diminished and I was on my way to being free of him. I would like to add that, throughout this experience, I sent loving thoughts to my ex-partner, wishing him happiness in everything, including finding a new mate to enrich and complete his life. This was vitally important to me at the time and always is in this type of situation. I knew there was no way that I could attract happiness into my life if I were harboring angry, jealous, or unloving thoughts toward anyone else. Like does attract like! More on this law later.

The Burn Up Method

This technique requires that you write the negative thought or thoughts on a piece of paper and then—carefully, very carefully—you set fire to the sheet of paper. You literally burn up the negativity. This must be done with great care or you'll have more than a negative thought to deal with. Best to do this exercise over a large ashtray, sink, or the toilet bowl so you can drop the paper as it gets close to your fingers and then quickly smother, drown, or flush the offending thoughts right out of existence.

I use a variation of this technique on a regular basis. When I wake up in the middle of the night with my mind going wildly crazy with worry thoughts, I write them all down on a pad which I keep on the bedside table. Once they're on paper, I can relax, knowing they're documented and that I

won't forget them and can deal with them at a more appropriate time. the next morning, in addition to being almost illegible, many of the notations are almost laughable in their lack of importance.

Nevertheless, in the middle of the night it is imperative that I get them out of my mind and on paper so I can go back to sleep. The next day, I take appropriate action in regard to my notes. For example, if I remember that I neglected to pay my credit card bill, I immediately write a check. Or, if I realize my library book has expired, I either renew it or return it the next day. Remember, I said that many of these nagging middle-of-the-night worries are inconsequential! Then, after I take appropriate action, I tear the paper into tiny bits and flush them down the toilet while mentally visualizing all worry thoughts swirling away into oblivion.

Recite Your ABCs

This is a variation on the above and one I use more than any other for middle-of-the-night worries. This differs from the others in this list because this is not a technique for getting rid of thoughts, but one for retaining thoughts. It has been very helpful to me so that is why I choose to include it here. As you have probably guessed, I am a great middle-of-the-night worrier. If prizes were handed out for such an activity, I'd be sure to win hands down. So, from first-hand experience, I gladly pass along this sleep-saver.

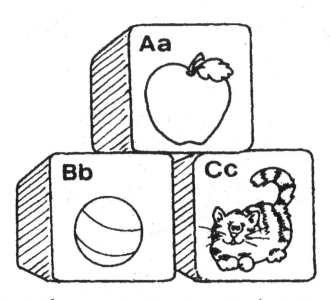

Here's the scenario: I wake up in the middle of the night with what at the time seems like monumental concerns, normally in the "Oh my God, I've forgotten all about [fill in the blank]" variety. If I don't happen to have paper and pen handy or I don't want to wake up enough to write, I lie there for hours assuring myself that I'll not forget. Naturally, this results in total wakefulness.

Here is my solution to this problem. I recite my ABCs. Years ago, I assigned a word to every letter of the alphabet: A is for apple, B is for ball, C is for Cat, and so on throughout the alphabet. Use words or images that you can and will always remember. Your personal alphabet will always remain the same once you decide which words you want to use for each letter of the alphabet.

Let's assume I have the following concerns or worries. 1) suddenly remember that my estimated tax payment is due on the fifteenth and here it is, the thirteenth. I need to get it off in the mail, pronto. 2) My hair appointment, which I made six weeks ago, is scheduled for this coming Friday. In the meantime, a lucrative speaking engagement turned up for this weekend. If I don't cancel the hair appointment sufficiently in advance, my stylist will never give me another appointment and I may even be charged for a late cancellation. I must call and cancel first thing in the morning. 3) I'm out of heartworm tablets for Charlie, my dog. How could I forget? Poor guy, I don't want him to get sick. Absolutely must pick up a new prescription at the vet tomorrow.

Here's how I remember these three worries so I can go back to sleep and still be sure I'll remember them in the morning. I recite my ABCs. "A is for apple," so I relate worry number one to an apple in some way. My number-one worry on this particular night was making my estimated income tax payment. Therefore I must associate my tax payment to an apple.

So, I visualize an apple wrapped in an income tax form perhaps, or I picture my payment check attached to an apple with scotch tape. My second worry was canceling my hair appointment in sufficient time to allow my stylist to reschedule. "B is for ball," so I visualize throwing a ball against the door of the salon or even at the stylist if that creates a better mental picture. My third worry was remembering to get a new heart-worm prescription for Charlie. "C is for cat" so I picture my dog Charlie and our cat fighting over the package of heartworm pills or perhaps I mentally see the cat stashing the sealed box in one of her secret hideaways. When I've made the three associations, I can relax confident in the knowledge that, in the morning, all I have to do is recite my ABCs and I'll remember all the worries that threatened to keep me awake. Interestingly enough, once I take care of the three worries, I mentally erase the ABC blackboard, so to speak, and my alphabet is ready to go to work for my memory once again with any and all new worries that are liable to crop up.

Wild Blue Yonder Maneuver

In this exercise, you recognize the negative thought, mentally remove it from your mind, and place it in your imaginary hot air balloon. Put in one thought at a time or as many thoughts as your balloon can handle in one trip. Then, prepare for takeoff and let the balloon ascend into the wild blue yonder, never to be seen or heard from again. Up, up, and away go the offensive thoughts in your mental balloon. Let it keep on going until it's out of sight and, along with the negative thoughts, out of mind.

The Blow It to Smithereens Method

If you have hawkish tendencies, if you like loud noises—even imaginary ones—or go for violent movies, this may appeal to your wilder instincts. In this case, you put the offending thoughts into your mental garbage can and, when it's as full of negativity as you deem appropriate, you simply blow it to smithereens. Puff. Bang. All gone. Demolished. Of course, with this as with all the other methods discussed, you have to keep at it. One single mental explosion may not do it. Persistence is the key!

The Golden Key

Some of the above methods may sound silly. Never mind; they all work. Pick the method that works best for you. I have one more method to offer that is not silly or off the wall. It is my favorite, it always works, and it can apply to any situation, problem, or mental rut. Called the Golden Key, it was originated by Dr. Emmet Fox, an eminent metaphysician and prolific writer. He advocates use of this method when you're in trouble or when your mind will not let go of a problem. It is simplicity itself, and I herein quote the complete rule: "Stop thinking about the difficulty, whatever it is, and think about God instead." A brief, but comprehensive explanation of Dr. Fox's method is contained in his book, *Power Through Constructive Thinking*.

Don't ignore this powerful method. If you feel it may be too religious for you, Dr. Fox states, "You may hold any views on religion, or none. All that is absolutely essential is to have an open mind and sufficient faith in a positive outcome to try the experiment." If you prefer to omit the reference to God, substitute "a positive thought" or "a positive solution" instead. Or, and this may feel more appropriate to you, substitute the word good for God. This is often done by metaphysicians who use the terms interchangeably.

I've used the Golden Key in uncomfortable or threatening situations with good results.

Another aspect of the Golden Key is its ability to defuse a troublesome person or a difficult situation. According to Dr. Fox, all you need to do is think, "Now I am going to 'Golden Key' John, Mary or that threatened danger. Then, proceed to drive all thought of John, Mary or the danger right out of your mind, replacing it by the thought of God." As mentioned before, you should feel free to substitute the wording that feels most comfortable to you in this exercise.

According to Dr. Fox, "By working this way about a person, you are not seeking to influence his conduct in any way, except that you prevent him from injuring or annoying you, and you do him nothing but good." I believe this works. I've used it in uncomfortable or threatening situations with good results. At the very least, it can help you to control your temper in volatile situations. As in counting to ten, it gives you time to cool down and collect yourself, plus sending out good thoughts to troublesome people and events does have immeasurable beneficial side effects, even though they may not be initially evident.

I am so impressed with the power of the Golden Key that I have placed a small gold key on a bracelet that I never take off. The miniature key on my wrist is a constant reminder of Dr. Fox's "practical recipe for getting out of trouble" reducing worry, and eliminating negativity. And, it reminds me that the power that gave us the ability to think is always available to us at all times for solutions and answers if we would but use it.

Well, there you have seven ways of dealing immediately with those negative, worrisome, persistent thoughts you'd rather not have. You can start with these methods right now and continue to use them daily in conjunction with your Personal Power Plan, which you'll soon learn about and start to implement.

3

Personal Power Plan

An Age-Old Formula

Getting what you want out of life—-manifesting your desires—can be very simple. It's so simple that, when people are given the formula, most will scoff, saying: "Anything that simple won't work!"

It is simple. And it will work, but only if you follow directions and follow through. Listen to your scripted message daily.

> *Getting what you want out of life—manifesting your desires—can be very simple.*

You'll have complete directions on how to do all of this shortly. Remember, what you say to yourself is what you get.

Before we go any further, let me emphasize how important it is to carefully read and think about the following five steps. In a nutshell, these five steps constitute the basis of your Personal Power Plan or PPP. The plan is based on an age-old formula that works; it always has and always will. Don't try to absorb it all at once. Let me take you through the plan step by step. The following is an overview. In succeeding chapters, I'll go into the various principles in detail and explain how to easily adapt and integrate this formula into your life.

Formulate Your Ideas and Desires

Nothing has ever been achieved in life without first being an idea or desire—a thought—in someone's mind. Everything exists as an idea in the mind before it becomes manifest or visible to the eye. Your thoughts are things; they have vibrations and possess energy. They're invisible, of course, just as radio and television waves are invisible, but we all know of the reality and power of those invisible radio and television waves. Radio and television waves have vibrations and possess energy, just as our thoughts do, and they produce sounds and images that are readily available to us through our personal radios and television screens by the simple touch of a button.

If you can accept the comparison of your thought vibrations to radio and TV waves, perhaps it's not too difficult to understand and accept the power of your ideas and desires—your thoughts. Even though they're invisible, just like the radio and TV waves, it's important to understand that thoughts are things; they have vibrations and possess energy. They can produce a desired end result for you just as radio and television waves produce their end result, sounds and pictures. A book was an idea in the mind of its author long before it appeared on your bookstore shelf; a building was a thought or blueprint in the mind of its architect before it became an edifice; an invention was a creation in the mind of the scientist who invented it before it became an actuality; an overture was music in the mind of its composer before it was heard by the public; a recipe was an idea in the mind of the chef who cooked it before one could taste the completed dish; and a gown was a creation in the mind of the designer before it could be worn or modeled.

Take a moment to think of some of the ideas or desires you'd like to see become realities in your life. Know that you'll soon be on the way toward realizing these goals, desires and accomplishments. Here's an interesting exercise that will serve to make this clear. Look around you. Notice everything in the room in which you're sitting while reading this book. The chair or couch on which you're sitting was an

Take a moment to think of some of the ideas or desires you'd like to see become realities in your life.

idea in someone's mind before it became a piece of furniture. The same applies to the table and the lamp beside your chair, the rug beneath your feet, the pictures on the walls, the walls that make the room, and the building itself. Realize that everything that surrounds you was originally an idea in someone's mind. Things do not appear out of nowhere. Everything must have a beginning. Every beginning is a thought, idea, or desire. Now expand your horizon. Look out of the window and notice the car in the driveway, the bicycle and the roller skates on the porch, the barbeque and patio furniture in the yard, the newspaper at the front door, the garbage can at the curb. All of these were ideas in someone's mind before they went through the stages of design, development, manufacture, and other necessary phases that finally brought them to manifestation or completion.

This exercise can go on almost indefinitely. Step out of the confines of your house or apartment and examine your neighborhood and community. Note the shops offering an endless variety of merchandise and services. Observe the schools, parks and playgrounds in your area. Look at the government buildings and business offices, the theaters, restaurants, beauty shops, and gas stations. All of these businesses, enterprises, services, and institutions were ideas before they became actualities. If you want to go further, utilize whatever means of transportation suits you, real or imaginary. Cars, trains, planes, and subways, motor homes and motorcycles, bicycles, scooters, skateboards, and roller skates all began with a thought in someone's mind as did the roads, highways, and by-ways that accommodate these various

Your desire, planted in your subconscious mind, properly nourished by repeated affirmations, will result in the manifestation of your desires.

means of transportation. And if, in your actual or imaginary travels, you end up in the country, the desert, or the mountains where there seems to be little or no civilization and man-made creations, don't think this exercise is over. Observe the trees and wildflowers, the insects, birds, and animal life. Look into the skies at the sun, the moon, and the stars. Note the clouds, the rain, snow, and wind. Where do you think all of these things originated? In mind, of course. Universal mind, the mind of the Creator.

A line from a famous poem comes to mind: "Only God can create a tree," as well as the saying, "Big oaks from little acorns grow." The acorn is the idea in the mind of God, the oak tree is its manifestation. Desire is the seed; it contains the nucleus necessary for manifestation. Your desire, planted in your subconscious mind, properly nourished by repeated affirmations, will result in the manifestation of your desires. Do you now understand the absolute power and possibility of this all-encompassing principle? Do you now see that everything exists as an idea in the mind before it becomes manifest? This very principle most definitely applies to the state and condition of your life. There are no exceptions. If your life has been confused and nonproductive up to this point, it is because your ideas and desires have been confused. Your ideas and desires have not been focused. Or you have constantly changed your focus before your ideas and desires had a chance to take root and grow and become real. Or you have been programming your mental computer improperly with faulty ideas and wrong goals. Remember: garbage in—garbage out! All of this must—and will—change.

Script Your New Life Plan

Here is where you write your life plan the way you want it to be. Not the way it is or always has been but the way you want it to be. You input the ideas and desires that are uniquely yours into every segment of your life: mental, physical, spiritual, family and relationships, career, and financial. This is so important that I will repeat it. You must put the ideas and desires that are uniquely yours in every segment of your life in order to have balance. Balance is all-important; without it, your life cannot become the well-rounded, happy, and

success-
ful ex-
perience
that you
wish it
to be.

Too much emphasis on your career is apt to put stress on other equally important areas of life such as your health, and/or your relationships.

Too much emphasis on your career is apt to put stress on other equally important areas of life such as your health, and/or your relationships. How many times have you heard of extremely successful or powerful individuals who make it to the top but in the process alienate their family or make themselves ill? By the same token, if you go gung-ho on the physical aspect of your life at the expense of other areas and hang out at the gym all day, your career is liable to take a downturn or your personal relationships might torn sour.

All areas of life must be in balance if you desire true health, happiness, and success. Keep that in mind as you script your plan. In this step you take personal responsibility for your life choices; you can choose to change what you don't like and don't want. You can choose to input what you do like and do want. You'll be starting with a clean slate—a fresh script. You and you alone will plan and write your new life story to read the way you want it to be. To me, this is a very exciting concept.

It is tremendously exciting, but don't take it lightly. This is a major step. There's no rush; you can take as long as is necessary to write your script. And you can relax in knowing that it's not written in concrete; you can revise it at any time. To avoid confusion and delay in the manifestation of your desires, however, it's wise to script your basic plan with care. Don't be frivolous; this is serious business. Try to put your major goals and desires down on paper the first time around. Then, you can simply modify or make changes as necessary when your goals, needs, or desires change. Obviously, you'll want to update your plan as goals and desires manifest or are accomplished, or as your focus and aspirations change.

In later chapters I will explain step-by-step how to determine the goals in every area of your life and exactly how to put them down on paper.

Record Your Script

In this step you affirm your scripted statements. You word the script of your new life plan in a positive manner in the present tense and you affirm that your scripted desires have already been received or accomplished. In later chapters I will explain how to do this properly, making the process easy to understand and execute. Don't become overwhelmed reading this. Remember, it is easy—very easy!

After your script has been written and affirmed to your satisfaction, it's time to audio record it. You can do this yourself. It, too, is very easy and I'll tell you exactly how to do it in the coming pages. Listening to your own voice will maximize the effectiveness of the program. An equally effective alternative, if you don't care to personally record, is to have your script

Listening to your own voice will maximize the effectiveness of the program.

recorded for you by someone you trust, such as a friend or family member, or by someone whose voice demonstrates trust and confidence to you.

Allow Your Desires to Germinate

You must listen to your personal recording and follow other important aspects of your program daily for a specific period without fail. This is the germination period. The positive thoughts being planted in your mind need time to take root, grow, and flourish. The nourishment they require will be provided by repeated listening to your personal recording and your unwavering belief in the outcome.

Your subconscious mind, which is your obedient, unquestioning servant, will bring forth the fruits of this mental action. Often the ways, means, and results will surprise you. Patience, persistence, and an attitude of positive expectation are essential. Energy follows thought, and when your thoughts, as directed by your recorded script, are flowing in a positive manner in the direction determined by you, you will get positive results. Changes will appear in form or experience.

Belief and faith are essential. When you plant fruit or vegetables in your garden, you believe that you'll harvest the crop that you planted, not other fruits or vegetables. There's no question about it. You have faith that, for example, where you planted tomato plants, you will get tomatoes; where you planted corn, you will get corn, and so on. You just know that if you do everything right according to the gardening books and advice from experts in the field, you will have a harvest of whatever you planted, not something you did not plant, at the right time for it to appear. You also know that you cannot expect to harvest to-matoes in your garden if you dig up the tomato plants and plant beans in their place; nor can you pull up the beginnings of your corn crop and put squash or any other seeds in the ground in-stead and expect to have a crop of corn. It simply doesn't work that way.

You cannot dig up the seeds you planted to examine their progress, or plant new or differ-ent seeds in place of the original ones, and still expect to reap the original harvest. You must simply plant and nourish and have total faith and belief in the outcome—without changing or interfering—and the crop you planted is assured you. This is a fact of life, a basic law. Do not con-fuse faith with hope. Hope is wishful thinking.

Properly applied, faith cannot fail. As Paul said, "Faith is the substance of a thing hoped for, the evidence of a thing unseen." Believe, have faith, give thanks in advance, and the substance will manifest.

Dorothy, the heroine in the Wizard of Oz, was brought up on a farm in Kansas. She argued with me about this concept. She said that any farmer will tell you that uncontrollable acts of nature also determine the outcome of a crop. True. The key phrase that I am emphasizing here is this: '"The crop you planted is assured you." Corn begets corn, beans beget beans, and so on. You will only get what you planted, not something other than that which you planted. If you are a farmer and you experience a tornado, a freeze, or other uncontrollable act of nature, you must replant. You must replant what you want, hope, and expect to get. And, if you run into a temporary snag in your mental programming, you must replant the thoughts you want to manifest, that's why this program stresses repetition. For the most part, farmers have no control over acts of nature. You do have control over your mind.

You will only get that which you planted, not something other than that which you planted.

This principle applies to the thoughts you plant in your mind via your personally scripted recording. You must believe and have total faith that the desired outcome will manifest at the appropriate time. The age-old quote, "According to your faith be it done unto you," applies as well today as it did thousands of years ago.

The most exciting thing about this whole process is that you will be tapping the powers of the universe to accomplish your goals. As amazing as this may sound, it's absolutely true. Because thoughts are things that have vibrations and possess energy, they do go out into the universe—we don't know where, but that doesn't matter. You will experience the results of this phenomenon in mysterious, often serendipitous, ways. At just the right time you will meet just the right person to help you with a certain need; you will receive a brilliant insight or the solution to a problem you've been struggling with; you will find yourself in the right place at the right time; you may even find yourself the lucky holder of a winning lottery ticket! Yes, the powers of the universe will be working on your behalf if you have faith and believe and persevere in your plan!

Maintain on Attitude of Gratitude

We all were brought up to say thank-you. If you knew someone, something, or some power was working on your behalf, wouldn't you be grateful? Wouldn't you have an attitude of gratitude? Yes, if you believe, have faith, and give thanks in advance, the substance, or that in which you had faith, will manifest!

In stating our affirmations, or script, we begin at the end, so to speak. We state our affirmations as if we have already received or achieved what we stated as goals or desires in our script. If we have already received or achieved everything we've stated or asked for, thanks are definitely in order. Therefore, it is imperative that we maintain an attitude of gratitude. Anything less will impede our progress toward our goals and could possibly dissipate the entire plan.

Perhaps psychologist William James was thinking of the as if principle when he stated: "You do not sing because you are happy, you are happy because you sing." Think about it. Which came first, the chicken or the egg?

4

How Does Your Garden Grow?

Law of Cause and Effect

Remember that old nursery rhyme, "Mary, Mary, quite contrary, how does your garden grow? With silver bells and cockle shells and pretty maids all in a row?" It sounds as if Mary had an organized, well-tended garden. How does your garden grow? I'm referring to your mental garden, of course. Is it organized, orderly, focused? Or is it like most of our mental gardens—in need of much weeding and a great deal of upkeep and clearing out. Is it, in fact, a total mess?

If you allow your mental garden to become overrun with unruly weed-thoughts—worry, doubt, fear, confusion, and apathy:—you'll soon find these energy-sappers have totally taken over.

If you allow your mental garden to become overrun with unruly weed-thoughts—worry, doubt, fear, confusion, and apathy:—you'll soon find these energy-sappers have totally taken over. There's no longer any room for your goals, ambitions, aspirations, needs, and desires to take root, sprout, grow, flourish, and, ultimately, to produce.

I'm comparing our minds and our gardens because the analogy is the easiest way to contemplate and understand the law of cause and effect—also referred to as the law of sowing and reaping. Of the many laws that govern the universe and our existence, it is the most powerful. Some call it the master law. Although all of the

laws work together and often overlap, this is the law from which all others flow. It has precedence over all of the laws. Essentially, the law of cause and effect means that, for every effect, there must be a cause or set of causes. Nothing happens by accident. Nothing. This is an orderly universe. There is a cause behind every effect—there is a reason behind everything that happens.

Let's go back to the garden analogy for a moment. Suppose you decide that you want a lovely, prolific garden so, first of all, you look over the area that you have to work with. Then you make a plan for your garden; it may be simple or complex. You may determine that you'll plant fruit and vegetables in one portion of your yard and put plants and flowers in another. Or, perhaps you decide to plant flowers and shrubs in the front yard, fruit trees and vegetables in the back.

There is a reason behind everything that happens.

You go to the nursery to buy the desired seeds and seedlings, and then, according to your plan, you put them in the predetermined areas. You carefully follow the directions on the packets of seeds, books on gardening, and the advice given you by the experts at the nursery. You maintain a mental picture of your garden in your mind. Regularly, and with total faith in the outcome, you tend your garden, watering, fertilizing, and weeding out intruders or unwanted growth. Because you have total faith in the outcome—after all, you can see results in a few short weeks when you garden—you don't feel obliged to dig up the seeds or roots to see how things are progressing.

After tending your garden with diligent care, at exactly the right time according to nature's timetable, you see the fruits of your labor. Your garden grows exactly as you planted it. Does this surprise you? It shouldn't if you've ever done any gardening, *What you sow is what you reap.* you know that where you plant, or sow, flower seeds of a certain variety, you will reap flowers of that variety and no other. What you sow is what you reap. The same law applies to vegetables, fruit trees, bushes, shrubs, and all other growing and living things. The law of cause and effect is an immutable law; it applies to everything in the universe. Therefore, it applies to your mental garden as well as to that garden in your front or backyard. What you plant is what you get. What you sow is what you reap.

Many years ago when my two children were young, they decided to plant a garden in our front yard to surprise me. When I arrived home from work on the day of the planting, they told me with great excitement about the beautiful garden they had planted. I don't know whether they bought or were given the seeds, but they assured me it was going to be a gorgeous flower garden. With great anticipation, we waited for the plants to appear. Soon sprouts broke through the ground and the excitement mounted. Daily they watered, weeded, worried, and waited for the flowers they anticipated. Eventually we did reap a crop—a crop of corn! Yes, that is what they planted. We had a healthy crop of corn stalks standing tall in front of the picture window! To their young minds, seeds are seeds and all seeds produce flowers. They did not know about the law of cause and effect—that what you sow is what you reap. If you plant corn, you will get corn, not flowers.

Mental Gardens

Now let's look at how this law, the law of cause and effect, applies to our mental gardens. Our thoughts are the seeds that create our lives and circumstances, just as the seeds we plant in our gardens create the flowers, plants, fruits, and veg-etables that we eventually reap or harvest. Each and every thought, idea, or desire in our minds is cause of the eventual effect, or outcome. There is no escaping the effects of this law. Our past thoughts, attitudes, ideas, and desires and the actions resulting from those thoughts, attitudes, ideas, and desires are responsible for our present circumstances. It

Our thoughts are the seeds that create our lives and circumstances.

is essential to understand and accept this. You are not the victim *Your present thinking and state of mind this minute is determining your future.* of circumstances. It is the choices that you have made in the past, in your thoughts, attitudes, and state of mind over the years, that have brought you to this point in your life. That may be heavy, but accept it. Assimilate it and forget it. The past is over. What's done is done. You cannot change the past, but you can change your acceptance of it by taking personal responsibility for your present circumstances and state of mind. Then, in order to change your future, you must determine to change your present thinking. In fact, it is imperative that you change it if, in any way, you are dissatisfied with your life. Why change? Because your present thinking and state of mind this minute is determining your future.

About two years ago, I had the pleasure and privilege of hearing Ron Martinez deliver a powerful motivational speech entitled, *"The Alchemy of Success: Turning Losses into Wins."* Dr. Ronald Martinez was a former high school athlete who became a quadriplegic in a diving accident in his mid-teens. The story of how he overcame adversity to find personal and professional success was the subject of this moving and inspiring speech. Ron was an expert on enormous problems and losses and how to overcome and transcend the limitations that confront us. He told of his joyous pre-injury days, the four nightmare years that followed his injury when his entire life, as he knew it, was lost, and what he called the "mountain years," his years of acceptance and accomplishment. Ron never felt that he was a victim; he said we all suffer losses---the death of a loved one, the breakup of a marriage, a major career setback. He said misery brings lessons and there is potential for learning in every loss; that because of the incredible resilience of the human spirit, we all have the power to over-come these losses. Yes, it is a struggle, he said, but through the gems of wisdom learned, we grow the most.

Ron went on to tell of a mystical experience he had that ended his nightmare years. He was lying on his bed, as usual, when he felt a tremendous calm come over him. He looked up and saw in front of him a split screen. On the left side of the screen, he saw himself living out the rest of his life, paralyzed and feeling sorry for himself. It was a living death. On the right side of the screen he saw what life could be: college, degrees, a job, friends, dating, living life to the fullest. It was an emotional, powerful, almost spiritual experience. Ron chose to embrace life and thereby entered the final phase of his life, the mountain years. He said all of his life is about choices and decisions. Our futures are not preordained; we invent and create them with the thoughts we think and the decisions we make.

Ron went on to get his Ph.D.; he had a happy marriage and, as a psychologist, a thriving practice. You may wonder why I speak of him in the past tense. Ron died of cancer. When asked about his thoughts shortly before he died, with characteristic optimism, he told a friend that he was looking forward to kissing his grandmother, who played a major role in his life, and then he planned to go out and play baseball.

In his thinking, he had already cast aside his wheelchair and restrictive body. Ron took charge of his thoughts, his emotions, and his life. Ron was presented with a choice, as we all are. He chose to leave the nightmare years behind and begin his climb up the mountain. He reached the peak and lived happily and successfully there for over twenty-five years. If Ron could do it with all the strikes he had against him, so can you. Now is the time to get hold of your thoughts and start your climb up the mountain. You, too, can create a happy and successful life at the peak.

Your thoughts create your life. If past, negative thinking has resulted in present circumstances that are negative, you have the solution. Change your thinking. Starting right now, you can begin to change your future by changing your mind. Change your personal programming. Implement your Personal Power Plan as soon as it is

Your thoughts create your life.

scripted. Remember, your present thinking and state of mind now determines your future. If past negative thinking has resulted in present negative outcomes, present positive thinking will result in positive future outcomes. In planning and executing your PPP, remember, only you, not any other programmers in your life, choose the effect you wish to achieve. You are the only thinker in your mind.

Your choice is the cause. The effect or manifestation of your choice is the result. It is inevitable; it is the law. Some may say, "Laws are to be broken," and many man-made laws are broken daily. Some get away with breaking the law, others get caught. This does not happen with universal laws; they cannot be broken. If we break any of the universal laws, we will eventually pay the price. Since the workings of the laws are invisible for the most part, we may not take them as seriously as we should. One way to overcome this is to look at an example, a law with which we're all familiar and one that does have visible effects.

The Law of Gravity

The law of gravity is an ever-present law in effect in our lives. Daily we work with and respect the law of gravity because it never deviates. We know that if we let go of our cup of coffee in midair without putting it down on a table, it will fall to the floor, breaking the cup and splashing hot coffee over everything. We know that if we throw a ball up in the air, it will come down sooner or later depending upon the velocity with which it was thrown because what goes up must come down. We have all been brought up to respect the law of gravity. We know not to step off high places such as buildings or bridges if we care about our bodies and longevity. Regardless of age, sex, race, color—whoever we are and wherever we might be in the world—we will fall.

The law applies to the Golden Gate Bridge in San Francisco, the Empire State Building in New York, the Eiffel Tower in Paris and bridges and tall buildings all over the world. Gravity has no preferences; it applies to all equally, everywhere on this planet. Gravity, as with all the other universal laws, is constant and impartial. It always applies. As previously stated, all of the universal laws are interrelated, with the law of cause and effect being the master law.

Let's look at two of the examples mentioned above relating to the law of gravity. The cup broke and splashed hot coffee all over because the cup was not put down on a solid surface. Someone let go of it in midair. That was the cause. The effect was the broken cup and splashed coffee. In the case of an individual's demise or bodily injury due to falling or jumping off of a bridge or tall building, the cause is the falling or jumping, the effect is the impact of the body on the pavement or water below, resulting in almost certain death. As you can see, the law of cause and effect works in conjunction with the law of gravity just as it works with all of the other laws and in all areas of life. Sometimes the law of cause and effect can have unexpected repercussions. I include this amusing story from a column in the *San Francisco Chronicle* to illustrate that there are no accidents; there is always a cause for every effect.

In an essay on dinner party etiquette that appears in the latest issue of *Esquire,* John Berendt extrapolates the lessons in classic tales of classic dinners. In one, Berendt describes a dinner party, probably in the late 19th century, at which French playwright Victorien Sardou spilled a glass of wine. The woman sitting next to him spilled salt on the stain, and Sardou picked up some of the salt and threw it over his shoulder for luck. The salt went into the eye of a waiter about to serve him some chicken. The waiter dropped the platter, and the family dog pounced on the chicken. A bone lodged in the dog's throat, and when the son of the host attempted to pull it out, the dog bit him. His finger had to be amputated.

The law of cause and effect is active and working at all times in your life and affairs, in major as well as relatively minor areas. Everything you do and every thought you have is a cause. What happens as a result of your thoughts, which control your emotions and actions, is the effect. Every cause has its effect, every action its consequence. This may be frightening to contemplate in some ways, reassuring in others. It's frightening when the cause seems to be outside the realm of your control, but reassuring when you understand how your innermost thoughts and personal actions control consequences. Because you are in control of your life's causes, you have total control over your life's effects.

The Law Are Universial

What about when the cause seems to be outside
the realm of your control? Assuming you're a
good person, you may ask, "Why do bad things
happen to good people?" There may be no answer to that monumental question. It appears to
me that bad things happen to both good and bad
people alike just as good things happen to both
good and bad people alike. The laws are impartial. It rains on both good and bad people; the sun
shines on both good and bad people; the winds
blow on both good and bad people. Hurricanes,
floods, earthquakes, tornados, and other acts of
nature happen to both good and bad people. Acts
of nature are also impartial. Planes crash, ships
sink, accidents of all kinds happen to both good
and bad people. Unless there is a case of delib-
erate sabotage, for the most part, the forces that
cause these happenings are also impartial.

Anyone who has lived through a catastrophe, suffered a tragedy, or experienced a loss,
large or small, might say, "Are you telling me
that I brought that upon myself? That somehow
I caused it?" In most cases you obviously did
not choose to have such an experience; the cause
was outside of your control but, and this is the
important part, you always have the ability to
choose your reaction to the bummers that life
hands out to you. You can elect to blame God,
the world, and others for what happens. You can

become depressed and stay that way, continually crying and bemoaning your fate, or you can do something about it. You, and you alone, have control over how you handle tragic circumstances and major setbacks in your life. We're back to the law of cause and effect again. Your attitude, your state of mind, your thinking now become the causes of the future effects of your life. What you make of this future, the rest of your life, is your responsibility.

I speak from personal experience when I say this. My husband Campbell, a jet pilot, was a captain in the Air Force. One Christmas, when returning to the air base where we lived, his plane crashed, exploded, and burned. The cause was a faulty propeller; perhaps it was a case of metal fatigue. It fell off in midflight. I know this because the co-pilot, who survived because he was able to escape the plane before it exploded, told me so from his hospital bed. The prop fell off when they were in the vicinity of a civilian airfield that my husband knew well because he often landed his personal plane on that field. According to the co-pilot, Cam laughed and said something like, "No sweat. I know this field like the palm of my hand. We'll be able to pull off a crash landing, no problem."

In attempting to bring in the crippled plane for the landing, he noticed a trailer park, which he previously did not know existed, at the end of the runway. He needed the additional space occupied by the trailer park to execute a safe crash landing.

As the co-pilot later told me, in the final moments of his approach, when he suddenly noticed the park, there was nothing for him to do except to make an abrupt turn to the left just before touching down in order to avoid running into and through the group of trailers. This was the secondary cause that resulted in his fatal crash. As any pilot can tell you, you cannot execute such a maneuver and survive. The effect of the set of causes, the prop failure and the trailer park, was the death of my husband, my widowhood, and the fact that my children no longer had a father. As I mentioned earlier, for every effect, there must be a cause or a set of causes. And, as Herbert Spencer said in 1861 in *Essays on Education*, "Every cause produces more than one effect"

After the chaplain and my husband's commanding officer broke the news to me, they suggested that the children and I leave our home on the air base the following morning. I was told that they would see that all matters were taken care of and that my furniture and household effects would be shipped to me wherever in the country, or the world for that matter, that I cared to relocate. I was shocked and angry at such a suggestion. Not only had I just lost my husband, but I was asked to give up my home of three years, our longest assignment anywhere, as well as the close relationships I'd built up with fellow Air Force families on the base during that period. At the most vulnerable point of my life I was stripped of my security, my home, my support system, and my friends. I was told there was a waiting list for our housing unit, which was probably true, but was it really necessary that I exit the very next morning?

In retrospect, I believe that their apparent cruelty was a combination of the housing element and, more importantly, the fact that the Air Force did not want a grieving family on their hands, especially during the holiday season. Anytime there's a fatal aircraft accident, any number of wives pressure their husbands to give up flying status and the military didn't want our presence to exacerbate that understandable response.

The months that followed were very difficult while I struggled with the enormity of my situation and tried to find the answers to the major questions confronting me: where to live, how to support myself and my two children, and what to do with the rest of my life. In my generation, young women were brought up to be wives and mothers. We were expected to undergo some sort of higher education, but that was just to "finish" us, so to speak, and to expose us to appropriate young men on the campus or at adjacent schools so that we would meet, marry, and settle down to become wives and mothers.

Nowhere in my script did the word career appear. I came from a very traditional family and my husband continued that throughout our married life. Never in my born days did I ever expect that I would have, or want, to work or become a professional woman. I had never had a serious job and I had no practical experience that I could put to use. Suddenly, everything changed.

To my astonishment and dismay, I was in charge. Where before I was never encouraged to have an opinion, make a decision, or speak my mind about anything. I found myself a single parent, designated breadwinner, and decision maker for our family of three. It was apparent that I was in charge; not my parents, not my husband, but me, Alice, a scared little girl—at least that's what I felt like—at twenty-eight. I kept asking myself, "I wonder where we'll be, what I'll be doing five, ten, twenty years from now?" Looking back over the thirty-five plus years since that fateful Christmas, I wish I could have reassured that terrified, naive little girl that everything would work out just fine.

I didn't know anything about the law of cause and effect or any of the other universal laws at that time. But somehow I knew and realized that because I was in charge, I had to make things happen the way I wanted them to happen. I could not allow myself to become a victim of circumstances if I wanted to survive, be happy, and make a new life for myself and my children. I basically understood, without being told, that I had the power of choice and therefore control over my life and circumstances. Did I make mistakes? Yes, plenty. Do I still? Occasionally. But, because I now understand and work with the laws, any mistakes and bad decisions that I might make now are not as costly as they used to be. Along the way I liberally employed the law of expectancy, which you'll read about next, so that each chapter of my life became an adventure to look forward to. I really had a lot of fun, life continues to be a ball, and I'm looking forward to a lot more of the same!

A close friend of mine, Margaret, has a daughter who, unfortunately, had a similar tragedy in her life. Joanne's husband, John, was also a pilot; he had a private plane. John, too, had a fatal air crash while returning from a business trip. Joanne was left with a young daughter to raise. She did not have to leave her home or community of friends who rushed to her support. John left her very well off so she wasn't forced to find employment without experience in any particular field in order to support herself and her young daughter. Although John died over twenty years ago, Joanne has not recovered from the accident. She is still sedated much of the time and often has to be hospitalized for long periods. It is regrettable that Joanne has led a less than happy life since losing her husband. I do not know her well enough personally to comment on her situation; I simply know the facts.

I can only say, as I've said before, that we personally, not someone or something outside of ourselves, are responsible for our happiness. We have power over our lives because we control our thoughts. We are in charge of what we say to ourselves all day long. Our thoughts, our personal words to ourselves, are the cause; the emotions we perceive as a result, are the effects.

It is not too late for Joanne, or you if you're stuck in a nonproductive situation, to repossess your life. It's never too late. But it is an individual, personal thing. No one can do it for you. You must take the responsibility. Please don't make this a heavy thing. It's simply a fact of life. Just remember that the law of cause and effect, as well as all of the universal laws, are at work at all times. There is no escaping them. They work for everyone, the rich and the poor, the good and the bad, black and white, red and yellow.

The Law Are Impartial

They are impartial. Understand them, live with them, and put them to practical use in your life. Think about it. What else can you count on totally? You can count on these laws and apply them to your life. Work with them and they will work with you. They are everywhere and always in force. Just as our man-made laws are designed to bring order to our everyday lives, these laws were designed to bring order to the universe. To cooperate with these laws is to bring order and harmony to your life. Go with the flow. You know bet-ter than to try to drive the wrong way down a one-way

We personally, not someone or something outside of our-selves, are responsible for our happiness.

street; why buck traffic? Work with these invisible laws that govern and control the universe for the betterment of your life just as you work with the laws set out by your local and national govern-ments for the betterment of the country and its citizens.

I'd like to sum up this chapter on the law of cause and effect with this quote from Ralph Wal-do Emerson: "Shallow men believe in luck, be-lieve in circumstances: It was somebody's name, or he happened to be there at the time, or it was so then, and another day it would have been oth-erwise. Strong men believe in cause and effect."

5

Act As If

Law of Expectation

The law of expectation says what we expect—and believe—will materialize. What we believe becomes reality. A corollary is: A*ct as if* your expectation has already come to pass.

In her powerful classic, *The Game of Life and How to Play It*, Florence Scovel Shinn uses a fable to tell of the power of expectations. A poor man met a traveler along the roadway who gave him a gold nugget, telling him if he sold the nugget, he'd be rich for the rest of his life. The poor man believed the traveler but kept the gold, because it gave the him feelings of confidence and security. So he went to work, knowing he could sell the gold if needed, and eventually amassed a fortune.

Years later, wishing to pass along to another needy person the good deed he'd received to another, the now wealthy man gave the gold nugget to a beggar, telling him

The poor man became rich because he believed that the nugget was, in fact, real gold.

what the traveler had told him years earlier—that by selling the nugget we would be rich for life. The beggar did not believe the wealthy man, so had the nugget appraised and was told the nugget was not gold at all, but was only brass. Angry, he threw it away. The beggar remained a beggar for the rest of his life.

The moral of this story is that the poor man became rich because he believed that the nugget was, in fact, real gold. This belief created an expectation of a future free from financial worry, which prompted him to act as if he would become wealthy. In the acting—behavior—he created the future he expected, that he believed would come to pass. Whereas the beggar, who did not believe the nugget was gold, developed no expectation that he could become rich, so took no actions to do so, and remained a beggar.

Shinn sums up the story thusly: "Every man has within himself a gold nugget; it is his consciousness of gold, of opulence, which brings riches into his life. In making his demands, man begins at journey's end; that is, he declares he has already received: 'Before ye call I shall answer.' "

Suppose you play the lottery on a regular basis and every day you check the newspaper to see if you have the winning numbers. Lo and behold, one day you hit it big and all your numbers match the winning numbers! Imagine how you would feel? Excited, thrilled, overjoyed! You bet!

Knowing [believing] you would have soon have vastly more money would soon developing into an expectation of having wealth would surely change your thinking and behavior toward money and your previous financial problems.

If you believed the money was really yours and coming, you'd feel like a millionaire, before the first check even arrives. Expecting to have more money soon, you would think differently about spending the money you have now. Thinking you are wealthy, you would likely start behaving as if you are wealthy. Importantly, believing promotes expectations which create feelings that encourage acting as if the expectations are accurate. What we believe becomes our reality; we create what we believe.

Do you believe in psychics? Suppose a psychic told you that many good things were about to manifest in your life—the perfect relationship, a promotion, an inheritance from an unknown relative, an exciting adventure. How would you feel? If you're like most of us, you'd feel optimistic—have positive expectations.

If you believed the psychic, you'd feel optimistic—secure in the expectation that the predictions would come true. Encouraged by your expectation of success, you'd begin to act differently, as if you can bring about the positive predictions. By acting differently you change your life.

By contrast, suppose the psychic had given you a gloom and doom prediction. Your relationship will go through trying times, your job looks shaky, and your stock portfolio will take a nosedive. How does the gloomy prediction feel? Optimistic or pessimistic? If you believe the psychic, you'll believe the pessimistic prediction. Belief determines expectations, which shapes how we act. When we expect doom, we act as if doom is coming, thereby increasing the likelihood it will.

What we think and what we say to ourselves, we become.

Suppose, you arrive at the office, a social engagement, or go on a round of errands. Someone you know looks at you closely and says, "What's the matter with you? Are you feeling sick?"

Expectations influence what we do.

"I'm fine, why do you ask?" you reply. "Oh, you look kind of pallid; there's something about your eyes—"Never mind that it's just the new "natural" blush or eye-liner you put on this morning, all of a sudden, you start feeling weak, flush.

Your expectation of illness, the belief in the friendly diagnosis causes you to act as if you're coming down with something. Soon, you're sure you've got a fever and your throat is sore. Even if you're able to ward off your imagined symptoms, your day is ruined.

Years ago when I was "between assign-ments"—the broadcast term for looking for a new position—I took a summer job as a traffic school instructor. Traffic school is where we can elect to go if we get a traffic ticket for a moving violation and don't want it to appear on your driving or insurance records. The school was one of the first in the area based on the psychological aspects of driving behavior rather than stressing rules and regulations, the method usually used by the high-way patrol.

One exercise was called a guided visualiza-tion. It was directed toward the serious problem of driving while under the influence of alcohol. Class members were told to close their eyes as I read, quietly, from a prepared script. The story line took the class through an evening out with friends. Everyone is jovial as they celebrate a happy occasion. with lots of eating and drinking, laughing and joking. When the evening ends, the party participants pile into cars for the ride home. A terrible accident occurs, complete with gory details. I described every terrible aspect of the accident scene. With their eyes still closed, many class members actually cried. Occasionally, there were loud sobs, sometimes screams. One time a woman fainted.

As the story progressed and the tension mounted, expectation set in. The *participants acted as if* the story were real. They believed what they were hearing. They behaved as if it were true. It was quite an experience

Another example of the law of expectation is an account in Dr. Deepak Chopra's *Magical Mind, Magical Body* of an experiment conducted by Ellen Langer, a professor of psychology at Harvard Medical School. Langer advertised in the newspaper for 100 people who were over the age of seventy to participate in an experiment.

In the study she took the respondents to a retreat for ten days where they were going to play called *Let's Pretend.* They were to pretend, or act as if, they were living thirty years earlier in the mid-fifties. Langer structured an atmosphere reminiscent of the era and the participants were instructed to live, act, talk, and think as they did thirty years prior. Respondents were totally immersed in a fifties mindset. Magazines, music, movies,

Ten days of the collective change in perception resulted in a reversal of biological aging.

fashions, décor, everything about their surroundings, apparel, and atmosphere was authentic circa 1955.

After a ten-day period in the 50's environment, Langer measured physical strength, perception, and cognition—taste, hearing, and visual threshold—and biological markers such as hand grip, finger length, height, and weight. Langer found that ten days of the collective change in perception resulted in a reversal of biological aging by several years. The study suggests that the collective perception of people and their interpretation of what is happening to them actually causes biological changes in their bodily systems.

Did the people in the study remain biologically younger? No, they did not. After they returned to Boston, they gradually returned to their original states. Nevertheless, what an astounding phenomenon after a mere ten days! What if they had remained in the experiment for a longer period? Or, what if, upon their return to Boston they programmed themselves to continue thinking of themselves as more youthful, vibrant, and strong, acting as if they were thirty years younger?

Chopra says the crux of this story is contained in a saying from the ayurvedic tradition: "The only reason people grow old and die is that they see other people growing old and dying. And, what we see, we become. What we hear, we become. What we touch, we become. What we taste and smell, we become." What we think and what we say to ourselves, we become.

Chopra says that our bodies are the metabolic end product of our sensory experiences and our interpretation of these sensory experiences. He talks about the stages people expect to go through in life as they grow older such as menopause, retirement, going on the social security rolls, being called senior citizens, and entering retirement communities, perhaps even nursing homes. It is the commitment on a collective level to a reality of aging that we create, often subconsciously, that reinforces the aging process.

Act as if your expectations are already a reality.

Let's not get caught up in the collective commitment to aging, or any other commitment we don't want. Utilizing the law of expectation, we can choose. We can buy into the reality of aging or we can expect to remain youthful. Let's act as if we are youthful, strong, vital, and healthy. Remember, what we say to ourselves is what we get. To many, being older is not to be feared; it has many advantages. If you agree, you may want to affirm "I'm older and better", or "I'm older and wiser", "Every day in every way, I'm getting better and better".

You are in charge of your future. Keep these thoughts and examples in mind when you write your personal script and implement your Personal Power Plan. Through your PPP, you determine in advance the end product you desire. You are in charge of your future. Expect a glorious one. Act as if your expectations are already a reality.

6

Like Attracts Like
Law of Attraction

*L*ike attracts like. People are drawn to and tend to gravitate toward people, places, and activities that interest or attract them.

If you like where you live, what attracted you to your residence—the area, the people, the neighborhood, and the climate? Perhaps you have relatives in the vicinity. Maybe you were drawn by the schools for your children or that it's close to your job. Whatever the reasons, attraction played a significant part in the decision to locate where you did.

We gravitate to places where there are others of similar cultures, customs, backgrounds, and interests. That's why you'll find ethnic communities in almost every state of the union. There are groups of Germans, Italians, Scandinavians, Portuguese, Vietnamese, and many other nationalities living in such settlements all over this country. That's why there are Chinatowns, Little Italies, Germantowns, and Japantowns. They feel more comfortable in such environments because they are surrounded by people with similar backgrounds and interests. It's the law of attraction at work.

Let's look at your job, position, trade, or chosen profession. I am fascinated by how people end up doing what they do for a living. Some know almost from the start what they want to do. Life is clear cut for the child prodigies who play the piano, violin, or other instrument at the age of six. They don't struggle with the big question,

"What am I going to be when I grow up?" But what about the rest of us? We muddle around, go to college, take courses that interest us, and jobs that merely pay the bills while trying to determine what we want to do.

Eventually, we end up in a trade or profession by choice or happenstance. Often, we stay there because that's where our experience now lies. But there must be an initial interest. Often we get into a business, like food service, because our first job to pay the rent was as a dishwasher. Years later we've become a maitre d' or own an eating establishment, for example. Alternatively, we may love preparing food so choose to attend a culinary academy to become chef.

Powertful Principle

This principle applies to every occupation. Regardless of how we become involved, it is the interest or attraction keeps us there. We associate with others in our trade or profession. Most of our thoughts and activities revolve around the business or service. Usually our social life also revolves around our profession. Look at Hollywood, for example.

When I was in the broadcast business, that's all I cared about. I was so enamored with broadcasting that I often said—and meant it at the time—that I would gladly do what I did for nothing. I was astonished that I was paid for what I

loved doing. Broadcasting was my life. I ate, slept, and dreamed broadcasting. That's all I talked and thought about. Everyone I associated with was related to the broadcast industry. To others, my obsession with broadcasting must have made me a total drag to be around except that most people can relate to broadcasting's end products: radio and television. So, even if I talked shop, outsiders could relate because they listened to radio or watched TV. It was not as if I were involved in some obscure profession that was foreign to others.

Friends could relate when I discussed the production of my latest commercial; then they could listen to the finished product at home or on their car radios. Or, if I had a particularly interesting TV interview coming up, they could tune in to our channel to watch it. Those both in and out of the business enjoyed taking part in my brainstorming sessions that often resulted in new station promotions and contests. But basically, most of my friends were those with whom I worked day in and day out. We worked together and socialized together. We had similar interests and goals, which were the basis of our conversations and activities. We were in the industry because we were attracted to it

What about your interests? What are your hobbies? What do you do for fun? My friend Fern is a jeweler who handcrafts earrings, pins, and pendants. Because her interests lie in making jewelry and other handcrafted items, she associates with others with similar interests and talents. She attends a variety of classes, gives talks and demonstrations on jewelry making, and participates in crafts shows and fairs. It has become a business for Fern; her items are on display and available in many boutiques in the area. While we have many other things in common, hence our friendship, I do not have her kind of talent and do not participate in the activities that interest her the most. But, by the law of attraction, she is surrounded by those with interests similar to her own; the majority of her friends are artists and craftspeople.

My friend Hans is a marathon runner. He has run marathons in many parts of the country and a couple in Europe as well. When he isn't running marathons, he's running around the local lake or through the neighborhood. He maintains a regular training schedule and runs almost daily, regardless of the weather or where he happens to be. His running started out as a means of losing weight and getting in shape; now it's a way of life. After thirty-five years of service to the government, he took an early retirement so that he could run full time. Now, running is what he does.

Running may be a lonely thing, but thousands of people all over the world are runners. There's a huge industry built around this activity. There are runners' magazines, runners' clubs, special shoes and apparel for runners, as well as vitamin drinks and energy supplements compounded especially for the growing population of runners. The variety of running shoes alone is enough to boggle the mind and new designs seem to be coming out daily. When there's a major event, such as the New York City Marathon, millions of people become involved. Runners come from all over the world to participate. Hotels are filled to capacity, airlines are sold out, taxis and restaurants do a booming business. Marathoners are everywhere spending money and contributing to the economy. The streets and bridges along the race route are cleared of traffic, the police are out in full force, hundreds of volunteers are on hand to pass out water and clean up discarded cups, onlookers line up six deep to cheer the runners as they pass by, and the entire event from beginning to end is covered on national television.

Law of Attraction at Work

A marathon is a good example of the law of attraction at work. People from all over the world with a common interest gather together to participate in an activity—running—or event—a marathon—that attracts them. But you don't have to be an active participant to be affected by the law of attraction; you can also be an observer. Whether you're watching a marathon on the streets of New York or on your living room TV, you're watching because you're attracted to that event or activity.

You don't have to be on the team to enjoy the sport. You can take part either as a participant or an observer. There are far more fans than team members. Whether you're in the stadium or in front of the TV at home, you're watching because you want to. You're attracted to a particular team or to the sport in general.

Let's continue with more examples of the law of attraction. What cultural activities interest—attract—you? Do you enjoy the opera, the symphony, the ballet, or the theater? So do countless others in your community; that's why there are opera houses, symphony halls, and theaters filled with like-minded people at every performance. Do you like art exhibits, museums, author readings?

When you attend an exhibit or reading, or visit a museum, others with similar interests will be there as well. Why? Because like attracts like, of course. Many of us are attracted to various groups, clubs, and organizations comprised of others with similar interests. I belong to a small writers' support group that has been helpful and meaningful to me. There are only six of us in the group and, at our monthly meetings, we share our successes and frustrations and disappointments with the world of publishing. We cry on each others' shoulders and bolster each others' egos. We share resources and names of potential agents and publishers. We really care about each others' progress in this difficult field and we congratulate and celebrate with utmost sincerity when one of us has good news to report. When I received the initial call from a publisher to whom I had submitted the proposal for this book saying they wanted to make me an offer, I contacted the members of my group instantly. I knew that, of all the people I know in the world, they are the ones that really care and could relate to my excitement and exhilaration over selling my book.

There are clubs, groups, and organizations of all kinds, large and small. Years ago when I was an Air Force wife, I belonged to a military wives' club, which kept women like me optimistic and busy when our husbands were off fighting wars or otherwise away from home on assignment. We did all of the social things: we attended luncheons, teas, and receptions, played bridge and bingo, and put on fashion shows and raised money for worthy causes. We did volunteer work for two reasons: the validity of the work and to keep ourselves and our minds occupied. We were not alone; all of us wives were in the same boat. We kept up each others' morale and we consoled and

helped in every way possible when the worst did occur. It was because of my work as a Grey Lady volunteer at our base hospital that I initially took a job in a doctor's office after my husband was killed in a military aircraft accident.

My friend Hans, the marathon runner, and I decided to look into the field of public speaking. When he worked for the government, Hans spoke to groups in the US, Europe, and the Far East about technical matters as a part of his job. I had spoken into microphones for twenty years but not before live audiences. So we joined Toastmasters where we found other people attracted to speaking. Many wanted to make a decent presentation to sales staff or at the annual awards meeting. Others enjoyed speaking to organizations such as Rotary, Kiwanis, Lions Club, and other groups. Some were seeking to overcome the fear of speaking in front of people.

Toastmasters offers many opportunities for speakers of all calibers. Hans and I became active in our local Toastmasters where we entered a couple of regional contests and won a couple of trophies. We found speaking stimulating and soon looked for a more challenging speakers' group, which we found it in the National Speakers Association and quickly joined the local chapter. Because like attracts like, we found ourselves surrounded by others

We were surrounded by othes with similar interests.

with similar interests. The main difference between Toastmasters and members of the National Speakers Association, or NSA, is that Toastmasters speak mainly on a personal or nonprofessional level while members of NSA are, or aspire to be, professional speakers and, for the most part, the membership consists of those who are paid—

often handsomely—for their speaking expertise nationally as well as worldwide,

I've mentioned personal activities and interests to illustrate the like attracts like principle—the law of attraction. How has this law affected you and your life? Do you see that it's natural to be drawn to others of like interests where you live, work and play? The dynamic effect of the law of attraction operates every area of life. You will utilize it when creating and implementing your Personal Power Plan.

The law of attraction works on the invisible plane. We are a magnetic force. We attract people, events, and circumstances into our lives that are in harmony with our predominant thoughts just as a magnet attracts metal filings. What we think about and what we say to ourselves tend to manifest. That is, our predominant thoughts—even though invisible—produce a like-attracts-like effect.

The Law of Attraction is nonjudgemental.

Our thoughts produce events and circumstances in our lives on the visible plane according to their kind. If we think negative thoughts, we get negative results. Think positive thoughts, and we get positive results. Think good luck thoughts, we get lucky results. We can increase the amount of luck in our lives by expecting lucky things to happen. Just as the magnet attracts metal filings, we attract good luck and positivity. It is the law of attraction. What we think or say to ourselves is what we get.

What do you want in your life? If you no longer want negativity, fear, and hate, rid your mind of negative, fearful, and hateful thoughts. If you want love, compassion, and tolerance in your life, think and practice love, compassion, and tolerance.

Easier said than done, you say. Yes, it is hard to break long-established patterns. But don't worry. The Personal Power Plan will help you succeed. It is carefully structured to accentuate the positive and eliminate the negative.

It is important to remember that the law of attraction is nonjudgmental. It doesn't take sides. It is totally impartial. It simply operates. A word of warning: Don't blame the laws if things go wrong in your life. When a catastrophe such as a hurricane, tornado, flood, or earthquake hits, it affects everyone in its path, good and bad alike. The important thing to remember is that you are in charge of your reactions to any event. You are the only thinker in charge of the thoughts in your mind. You are responsible for the thoughts that control your existence.

Applies to Actions and Attitudes

This powerful law or principle also applies to our actions, attitudes, and emotions which, of course, are controlled by our thoughts. An easy-to-understand example is that of the smile-versus-frown facial expression. Go around with a frown or disagreeable expression on your face and watch what happens to those around you. They'll soon replace any smiles they may have had with equally sour expressions. It's the same as a dark cloud coming over a formerly sunny sky; suddenly everything changes. A frown is contagious.

So is a smile. Approach a harried sales clerk who is dealing unsuccessfully with a line of impatient customers with a genuine smile and watch the clerk's expression and demeanor change.

This is easy to see with small children. Picture a crying toddler upset over a stubbed toe. How do you get the child laughing again? With frowns and nagging? Of course not! The like-attracts-like principle dictates that the way to succeed is with a big smile, hugs, and assurances. Yes, smiles and frowns are contagious. Wear the expression you want to attract, for attract it you will!

The same principle applies to behavior. Agreeable people attract agreeable responses in those they deal with. Reasonable people attract reasonableness in their personal lives and business dealings. Generous people find generosity reciprocated. Stingy people find stinginess reciprocated. Hostile people attract hostility. Violent behavior produces violent results. Exude positive vibes to attract positivity to you. Exude negative vibes and attract negativity. If you don't like the way you're presently treated by family members, neighbors, friends, coworkers, clerks, bus drivers—anyone and everyone—examine your behavior and attitude.

Determine how you want to be treated by others, then act that way to them first. The law of attraction in these instances is interwoven with the law of cause and effect. Keep the law of attraction in mind when scripting your Personal Power Plan so that you will attract the people, things, and situations you desire into your life.

7

Expect to Receive
Law of Abundance

Our world is one of abundance. All I need do is step out into my backyard to experience the law of abundance in action. I have a plum tree, a pear tree, and a lemon tree. The lemon tree produces all year round. This single tree produces enough lemons on a continuing basis to amply stock produce markets within a five-mile radius. The more we pick, the more it produces. I am abundantly supplied with lemons. Fortunately, I like lemonade. The plum and pear trees also produce abundantly. Dealing with the ample crops each year becomes a major project during their limited season of production.

The fruit from these trees is a symbol of abundance to me. When one year's crop is gone, I know the life source within the tree will produce another crop the following year. The life source may be invisible, but it's always there within the trees. That is the important concept to understand. Even when the tree is dormant, when the fruit has dropped and the branches are bare, it is full of potential abundance. We do not have to see the life source in order to benefit from it. In fact, we often cannot see it. We must accept and believe that it exists. When we can do that, we will have a consciousness of abundance—a prosperity consciousness. When we achieve this state of knowing, we will always be prosperous.

Prosperity can be measured in many ways: by pride and *The law of abundance works through consciousness in direct accordance with our belief in it and expectation of it.* joy in our family, material comfort, a flourishing career, good health, and vitality. For many, prosperity is frequently measured in material things: homes, cars, boats, clothes, jewelry, investments, possessions—anything and everything that money can buy. These things, like my lemons, pears, and plums, are symbols. The source of these symbols is our inner consciousness of abundance— our prosperity consciousness.

Our personal life source is within—within our creative, thinking mind! The law of abundance works through consciousness in direct accordance with our belief in it and expectation of it.

Surrounded by Abundance

Consider what we take for granted, yet cannot live without: air, sun, water, and the earth itself in which we plant things that sustain us. There is plenty for all of us. People are often packed like sardines in stadium filled to capacity for a sporting event; a rock concert featuring a well-known star. Yet, there's enough air for everyone. We take this important resource for granted, but we couldn't survive without it.

What about food and the starving millions around the world? Shocking as it may be to contemplate, there is enough food to feed all. Our government pays farmers to destroy crops to keep prices up. Some crops die because there aren't enough workers to harvest them. Food is often warehoused until it spoils. Supplies shipped to Third World countries frequently never reach those for whom they are intended. Even during the Great Depression there was no lack of food in this country. Much was stored in granaries and warehouses. Distribution was and continues to be a problem, not the lack of food.

Money is not evil; it is a means of acquiring what we need and want.

Consider the food supply in the seas and oceans, which could feed the population of the world. Like my lemons, there's an endless supply. When you get away from the city and out into the country, look around. Notice how lavishly extravagant nature is, almost to the point of wastefulness. There is enough for everyone. Cultivate a personal consciousness of abundance, and you will be abundantly provided for all of your life.

George Bernard Shaw said, "The lack of money is the root of all evil." Money is not evil; it is a means of acquiring what we need and want. Obsessing over money can lead to negative situations. Perhaps you heard, as a child, that it's sin-ful to be wealthy and have possessions, that poverty makes us better people. If you believe that, you've been programmed.

It is not a sin to be rich; it is a sin to be poor. Yes, the rich often get richer and the poor get poorer. Why? Because of their consciousness of being rich or poor. If you prefer being rich, it's essential that you acquire a consciousness of abundance. Abundance is our birthright. We must consciously and constantly think abundance. If you're presently suffering from lack, it's because your thinking has been focused on lack. Here the law of abundance is working with the master law of cause and effect. If you have a consciousness of lack, that is your cause. Consequently, lack will be your effect If you think or have a consciousness of abundance or plenty, that is your cause. Abundance, or plenty, will be your effect.

Expect to Receive

Just thinking of this infallible law and the effect it can have on your life should make you clean up your thinking act fast! Abundance is not only a monetary thing; it is also attitudinal. What do I mean by that? Do not think of abundance only in terms of money and possessions. We can be rich in these things and still be poor in our thinking, attitude toward life, and approach to the world. The law of abundance works

Having abundance is an attitude.

through consciousness in accordance with our basic beliefs. To enjoy true abundance, we must upgrade these beliefs to reflect our God-given potentials. Thoughts of poverty, in actuality or in spirit degrade; thoughts of abundance uplift

Someone once said, "What is plenty for one may be poverty for another." My favorite kind of TV programming is the interview show. I enjoy trying to find out what people are really like; what makes them tick. On several occasions, I've

What is plenty for one may be poverty for another.

heard celebrities who were known to have come from a poor background asked something like, "Wasn't it just awful being poor when you were a kid? How did you handle it??' The answer usually was, "We didn't know we were poor, so we were happy." As children, these people had a consciousness of abundance because they came from happy families. They may have been living at poverty level, but if they had an abundance of love, something many wealthy people lack, they had plenty. Happiness wasn't tied to money.

What is Money?

Let's explore further the concept of money. Just what is it anyway? Dollar bills? Checks? Certificates? Those are just pieces of paper. It's what these pieces of paper represent that counts.

The dollar bills supposedly stand for gold bars stashed away in the mint, the checks stand for money you have in the bank; the certificates can be bank CDs or represent stocks, bonds, or other investments. Is the gold really in the mint or have we printed too many pieces of paper? Is the money really in the bank or is it out on loan to someone else?

The certificates are merely pieces of paper that represent something you own. You can't actually put your hands on your ownership fraction of a mutual fund, for example. And what about your credit card and other charge cards? All of these things—the dollar bills, the checks, the certificates and the credit cards—are symbols of your abundance. The gold, the money in the bank, the holdings that the certificates represent, your good credit represented by your credit cards, are invisible. They're invisible but you have faith that the source is truly there. Remember my lemon tree. Because you know you have money in the bank, you feel abundant. You don't walk around with your net worth actually in your purse or wallet. We rely on symbols.

I normally keep only about twenty-five dollars in my wallet. If I'm on vacation or traveling, I usually carry traveler's checks. Cash makes me nervous. I'm more frugal with cash than with checks or plastic. But I'm never concerned about a lack of money just because I only have twen-

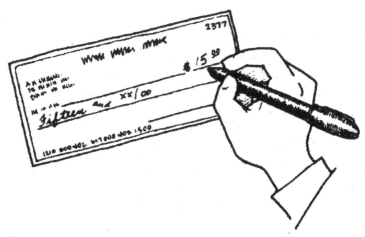

ty-five actual dollars on my person. I trust my symbols—my checks, and my credit cards—to take care of my needs. I rely on the source, the bank, and my good credit. I have a consciousness of abundance and I live with that knowledge; therefore, I am wealthy. It is a state of mind.

I used to grumble about paying bills, especially taxes. Then it hit me that I'm privileged to live in the greatest country—so what am I complaining about? Now, when I mail in my estimated taxes throughout the year, I say, "Thank you for this country, my home, and my standard of living." I have to send the checks anyway, and I am grateful, so why not express it? To show my appreciation for the privilege of living where I do, I put hugs and kisses on my checks!

Yes I do! Instead of putting "no/100" at the end of the line where you write in the dollar amount, I put "xx/00." Yes, I send my checks with hugs and kisses! I got such a kick out of the symbolism of that, that I now do the same with all of my checks. It's in appreciation to my creditors for their faith in me. It's my way of saying thank you for loaning me money, as in mortgage or car payments, or in issuing me credit as do my utility companies and department stores. More importantly, it reminds me that the source, my good credit, is always there, even if it's invisible.

This has worked well for me. You might want to try it. In talking about this subject with friends over dinner recently, I was given some other ideas to increase abundance and prosperity consciousness. Allen said he carries a one hundred dollar bill in his wallet at all times. He has never spent it, but every time he opens his wallet and sees it, it makes him feel prosperous. He knows it's there and his to spend anytime he wants, and it gives him a good feeling. And you are never broke with one hundred dollars in your wallet.

Allen also confided that he and his wife had an ongoing thing about money. He tended to be frugal while she enjoyed spending; keeping the money in circulation, she called it. He said it was uncanny, but every time they went for a walk, she always came across coins lying on the ground. She was certain that the universe does provide if you have faith, if you have a consciousness of abundance. Have you found any pennies from heaven lately?

Susan, at the same dinner party, told us about one of her abundance techniques. She loves beautiful, unusual wallets and small money purses and she enjoys buying expensive ones. They give her a feeling of prosperity. When she talks with someone who has a money problem, she instantly gives the person her newest wallet with the instruction that it is to be carried with a spirit of true abundance because that is what a beautiful money holder denotes.

Bob said that, in payment for a bill, he was given two hundred dollars in cash instead of the

check he requested. He wasn't used to carrying around that much cash but, as he said, it gave him a tremendous feeling of prosperity. To further that feeling, he decided to take himself out to dinner at a fine restaurant and order lavishly *Where does money— wealth—come from?* in a way that he normally doesn't do. He said the experience was a real high. It changed his usual thoughts of not having enough to that of having abundance. Without the desire or need to splurge again, he now carries two hundred dollars in his wallet at all times to reinforce his newfound feeling of abundance.

Do you, perhaps, have the feeling that there's only so much money to go around, and if you have more than what you consider your fair share, someone else is deprived? Or do you resent others who have more than you do and that you deserve some of their wealth? If so, rid yourself of those thoughts now and forevermore. Just as with the unlimited supply of air, sun, and water, the supply of abundance is unlimited. It is infinite. There is enough for everyone. There is an unlimited supply. Those with a prosperity consciousness will feel fulfilled; those with a poverty consciousness will not.

Where does money—wealth—come from? Money does not come from banks, safe deposit boxes, armored trucks, mattresses, tin cans bur-

ied in the yard, the stock market, or investments
of any kind. Money is put into these places. So,
where, then, does money or wealth come from?
It comes from the creative mind, from ideas that,
when instigated, produce wealth. Is there a limit
on ideas? No! Think of the abundance of creative
ideas, new inventions, innovations, and concepts
that have impacted the world in your lifetime. In
my life I've seen the advent of
Open yourself jet airplanes, television, and
to the flow of computers, to name three ma-
abundance. jor innovations. What has been
developed in just the past ten
years? What about the next ten
years? To repeat, money, wealth, and abundance
comes from the creative mind, from ideas. When
you possess a consciousness of abundance, creative ideas come to you.

Some will say hard work produces wealth. In
many cases, this is true. Hard work combined
with a prosperity consciousness can produce
wealth. But hard work alone, may only produce
frustration. How many hard workers do you
know who are wealthy? More likely than not, the
hard workers of your acquaintance are, or will be,
tired and discouraged by the time they retire and
collect social security, with little financial gain
to show for their many long years of hard labor.
Wealthy people, on the other hand, often do not
work as hard as their less affluent counterparts.

They work smarter. That is, they employ creativity and ideas, combined with a consciousness of prosperity, to propel them to the top and open them to the flow of abundance.

Open yourself to the flow of abundance. Believe you are worthy. Believe you have a right to be prosperous and abundantly supplied. Accept the good fortune that comes your way. Accept the riches and good things that come to you with gratitude.

8

Belief Becomes Reality
Law of Belief

The Law of Belief says what we believe becomes our reality. The law contains two vital words—believe and reality. Webster defines believe as "to have a firm conviction—to take as true and honest." Whereas reality is "a real event or state of affairs." Therefore, when we have a firm conviction about ourselves and believe it to be true and honest, it is likely to become reality—real in our lives.

Cause-and-Effect Process

Belief is the cause, reality is the effect. Recently, when flipping my TV dial, I came across a woman interviewing a panel of people who believed they were ugly and unattractive. They all looked like normal people of average good looks, to me. I did not see any one of them as unattractive. What mattered was that the people on that show truly believed, with all their hearts, that they were ugly misfits in a world

What we believe becomes our reality.

of beautiful people. They were so firmly convinced of this that their belief became their reality. A belief was reflected in their actions, body language, and attitudes, thereby substantiating it. They expected rejection and they received rejection.

By contrast, consider a quote from one of the world's most beautiful women, Sophia Loren: "Nothing makes a woman more beautiful than her belief that she is beautiful." Loren is indeed beautiful. How much do you suppose Sophia Loren's belief in herself contributes to her beauty, to her reality?

When a woman, a raving beauty or otherwise, truly believes she is beautiful, she will radiate beauty, so people say, "What a beautiful woman," commenting on her inner beauty. Further, she will likely learn how to highlight her features with make up, jewelry, and clothing. By contrast, a woman who believes she is ugly, will neglect her appearance. She will use make up poorly or not at all. She will ignore her hair, letting it become unflattering. She will dress in a manner that detracts from her attractive qualities.

Without knowing or realizing it, we put out vibes—invisible messages in the form of actions, body language, and attitudes—that reinforce our inner convictions. How do you feel and act when you believe you look great? Likely you project a strong image of confidence. Confidence is attractive. By contrast, how do you act when you do not feel unattractive? When feeling down and out, you likely project self-doubt, which is unattractive and off-putting.

Cultivate an Image of Beauty

I had a great aunt who I thought was a real beauty. She thought so as well—an assurance that was reflected in all that she said and did. I'd heard of her many romantic conquests. One time I took a male friend to meet Aunt Click who was then in her nineties. Batting her eyes, she become a scintillating women. My friend was actually smitten!

One time when reminiscing with relatives about her, I mentioned her beauty. Another aunt who knew Click well remarked, "Beauty? No, she was quite ordinary looking." I was stunned. Later I pulled out an old photo album to find snapshots of Aunt Click. Sure enough, Aunt Click may not have been the extraordinary beauty I remembered, but she was far from ordinary looking. In every photo she exuded an unmistakable air, a mystique; she radiated beauty from every pore. She had a firm belief that she was beautiful and therefore she became beautiful.

Aunt Click had a firm belief that she was beautiful and therefore she became beautiful.

Maria Riva, in an interview discussing her biography of her famous mother, Marlene Dietrich, alluded to that same inner belief: her mother's total conviction that she was an extraordinarily beautiful and sensuous woman which, of course, she was. How much was true and how much did Dietrich cultivate through her inner belief combined with her desire to create a legend?

My mother was a petite woman, who everyone thought was adorable because she was like a little doll. They called her Dolly. But Mother did not believe that being small was beautiful. In fact, she truly considered her small size as a real disability. Her constant lament was, "It's so hard being short. I can't reach anything that normal people can, my feet never touch the floor when I sit on chairs, and I can't buy clothes; everything has to be altered."

Her belief that she was abnormally short became a conviction. Not surprisingly, she found life difficult. I know many people as short as Mother, and never heard any of them complain about their lack of stature. I'm sure that they, as I do, often have to stand on a stool or chair to reach things in closets or the kitchen. So what? And, until I discovered petite sizes, I always had to have clothes altered. I still have to shorten most sleeves and hems. But I don't consider being short a problem; in fact, I kind of like it. I prefer being on the short side rather than on the tall side.

This is not a criticism of my daring mother; on the contrary. I wish that I had known earlier that belief creates reality. Perhaps I could have helped her appreciate and enjoy her uniqueness. There is much to be said for being small—comfort in airline seats, for example. Importantly, Mother was the perfect size for my Dad, who was not a tall man.

Concern about size is not unique to women. Men can become obsessed with their height, for example. There's a stereotype that short men feel pressure prove themselves. Do they believe that because they're short they have to be aggressive, extroverts, or macho—attributes that eventually become their reality—in order to be manly or accepted?

What do you believe about yourself and how do these beliefs affect your reality? Julius Caesar said, "Men willingly believe what they wish." My friend Ed is on the short side. I don't know his actual height, but I'm fairly certain he would gladly accept an additional two or three inches. However, rather than letting his shorter stature defeat him, Ed chose to think positively about it. His affirmed: "Think tall", became part of his life. "Think tall" cards were posted on his desk, car dashboard, and in his wallet. He signed notes with, "Think tall." He told himself he was tall. He felt tall. He walked tall. To me, he was tall. He had a tall attitude. He came to believe he was tall and so, for all practical purposes, he was.

What Are Your Beliefs?

How have your beliefs created your reality. Explore this powerful process now because your health, happiness, prosperity, and success—your realities in life—are, in fact, firmly rooted in your personal beliefs.

Being a student and a teacher of the power of personal programming, I thought I had my thinking, my beliefs, on track. However, upon self-examination, I discovered that I have a personal belief that is inconvenient, annoying, and sometimes even frightening. It's that I will get lost when driving or traveling, which emanates from my having a poor sense of direction. This distills to two beliefs: the belief that I have a poor sense of direction and the belief that I'll easily get lost.

I think sense of direction is inborn and I was born with a poor sense. So, when I set out for a new destination, I worry that I'll get lost. And I often do! I go from pedestrian to pedestrian calling out the window for directions. Of course I always do reach my destination, but I do so with considerable stress.

Of course I always do reach my destination, but I'd save myself much distress if I had the

inner confidence to believe that I will always find my way without problems. Having that assurance would make traveling more enjoyable, rather than one of anxiety and dread.

The Law of Belief

Do you allow yourself to enjoy life, or do you believe you don't deserve to enjoy yourself? This kind of guilt is prevalent; often it's left over from our big programmers, those authorities in our early years.

If you're suffering from left-over beliefs implanted by old voices from the past, it's time to stop that tape, reverse it, and wipe it clean. It's time to reprogram your mind with the thoughts, messages, and directions that you want to hear. It's time to reprogram your mind with positive messages that will get you what you want in life. As the Bible states, "According to your belief, it is done unto you." Make sure that what is done to you is of your choosing.

How do you uncover those old voices, and silence them? You can enter therapy to explore your past and the many ways your unhelpful beliefs took root.

While psychotherapy can be extremely helpful, it is time consuming—maybe years—and expensive. Just finding a qualified therapist to whom you can relate is a challenge as well.

Reprogram Yourself

My friend Kurt undertook his personal reprogramming. Kurt was, in his words, a fat kid.
He was overweight as a teenager and became
a heavy man. He expected to be heavy. It was
part of his belief system. Everyone in his family
was overweight. His parents believed that being
thin was sickly, whereas being overweight was
healthy and to be desired. Kurt weighed over 200
pounds when 160 pounds would have been a
more appropriate weight for his height and bone
structure. Because of his European ancestry and
upbringing, he ate rich, heavy meals.

It may have been a midlife crisis, a health
scare, or simply a desire to look and feel better
that led Kurt to personally undertake a change
in his belief system, which led to an exercise
program and change in diet and, ultimately, to a
tremendous change in his appearance. Kurt started jogging and bicycling on a regular basis. He
began working out at the gym to tone his upper
body muscles. In a matter of a few months Kurt
was at his ideal weight of 160 pounds. He looked
and felt years younger
than his fifty-five years.
When he looked in the
mirror, he said, "If my
mother could see me
now, she'd never be-
lieve it!" Kurt changed

*Reprogram your
mind with the
thoughts, messages
and directions that
you want to hear.*

his personal belief about himself, and that of his mother who believed he'd be roly-poly forever, to a new personal belief of being strong, lean, healthy, and attractive.

Kurt mentally and physically reprogrammed himself. Mentally, through positive affirmations about his health and body image, he changed his inner belief that he was and always would be fat to a new belief of being the healthy, attractive person he'd always dreamed of being. His new belief system required that he institute a physical regime, which he did. Through his mental and physical programming, Kurt's new inner belief became his outer reality.

Belief is insidious, creeping in and grabs hold of our selves; we unwitting become slaves to our beliefs. When I was shopping for a house, my belief system determined that I deserved to have a little vine-covered cottage rather than the grand, spacious home I truly wanted. I looked for a home for two years and finally, out of desperation and out of time, I settled on a vine-covered cottage. I looked at and passed by countless houses that, in retrospect, I would have much preferred. Why? My belief system told me I didn't deserve any of those grand houses; I deserved a little vine-covered cottage. I rationalized that I could only afford a house of a certain price even though friends, family, and my real estate agent told me otherwise. I ignored their advice and the figures they showed me; I believed I only deserved a house of a certain price and quality. For a small amount over the price I paid for the home I bought, I could have gotten my dream house. My belief system would not allow it. After all, who was I to have a gorgeous dream house?

I eventually spent ten times the price difference into my vine-covered cottage to make it into my dream house. Incidentally, part of my renovation was having the vines removed so I could see the house.

Avoid the Victim Trap

Have you, without realizing it, fallen into the circumstances trap? Do you believe that what's happened to you over the years has been *done to* you? Do you feel that you have nothing, or at least little, to say about your experiences, circumstances, and the events of your existence? Do you find yourself coming up with statements such as, "I hate my job but I can't quit or change *now*. I've put in too many years on this one; might as well sweat it out until retirement. Besides, what else can I do? What else do I know? I'm stuck, and that's the way it is." Or, "We're in a recession? Things are bad all over. Everyone's getting laid off. There's no point in even looking for a job." Or, "Sure I've got a lot to offer but I'm—too young, too old, under qualified, overqualified, black, a woman, disabled—for the job I really want." When you believe destructive mental statements, they are, or will become, true. What you say to yourself is what you become.

Maybe you've fallen into the victim trap. Victims think along these lines: "How can I be expected to succeed, coming from a dysfunctional family like mine? I couldn't do anything right then and I can't do anything right now!" Or, "Opportunities?

Sure, if you've got a college degree, or you know the right people, or you've got a line of bull. Me, I don't stand a chance!" Or, "Men (or women) just don't like me. Whatever it is that's wrong with me always puts people off. I'll never find anyone to love."

Whatever you say to yourself, if you believe it, you'll make it come true. The glass is either half empty or half full. Henry Ford said, "He who thinks he can, can. And he who thinks he can't, can't. This is an indisputable law." If you find yourself falling into this bottomless pit of negative belief, get out of it—Now!

Who and what you are, and what you will become, is a reflection of your current prevailing mental attitude. Is your attitude positive or negative? Do you have an attitude of superiority or inferiority? Are you friendly or unfriendly; loving or unloving?

These and the myriad other attitudes you harbor are reflections of your inner self, your personal beliefs. The good news is you can change your attitudes and beliefs. Even if you had the highest priced, most knowledgeable therapist, nothing would change without your consent and a

If you believe what you say to yourself, you'll make it reality.

great deal of work on your part. Now, with your consent and, more importantly, with your desire, plus the short time that it takes to institute your Personal Power Plan, you, personally, can change your belief system. You can change your life. Are you ready to get started?

9

Your Game of Choise
Arenas of Life

You may be thinking, "All of this makes sense, but how do I apply it? I want a concrete plan of action—solid action steps I can take. I want to get started right now. What's next?"

Life can be broken down into areas or arenas.

To achieve balance we must treat each arena of life equally, otherwise life is out of kilter. Next is to think through what is in each of your arenas to guide you in writing your life script so it is balanced and the way you want. Your new life script need not be the way it is, was, or always has been. Instead you will write a new script to be exactly the way you want it to be.

Life's Arenas

An arena is a place of activity, such as a sports arena where spectators watch a football game, for example. We can think of our important life's activities as taking place in a methaporical arena or place.

Mental

The Mental Arena includes education, both formal and informal. It includes reading to increase your knowledge of what interests you as well as  what you need or want to know more about. It includes writing you may do, personal or otherwise; writing is definitely a mental activity. It includes planning, analyzing, thinking, and studying. It includes learning a new skill.

Many activities in the Mental arena overlap other arenas. For example, actingAto increase your knowledge of skills helpful in your job may also fall in the Career Arena. Don't worry about in which arena to place multi-related activities.

What is important is recognize them and write them down.

Physical

The Physical Arena includes health, nutrition, exercise, image, and appearance. Health pertains to the condition of your body; it is supported by proper nutrition—what you put into your body, and exercise—what you do with your body. Without proper and necessary attention to the first three—health, nutrition, and exercise—your image and appearance will fare poorly. Image and appearance include your overall look: hair, makeup, wardrobe, and grooming, and your personal demeanor: your energy, vitality and the way you present yourself.

Spiritual

In Spiritual Arena are morals, ethics, and values. Deending upon your personal thoughts on these qualities, you may prefer to place them in the career arena. Your personal philosophy of life, which only you can define, goes in the spiritual arena. If you have an affiliation with a church

or a religious or spiritually oriented group, this is the arena for them. Here is where you put your connection with a higher power.

Relationships

The Relationships Arena is important. Family may include spouse and children in the traditional sense, as well as people you live with such as a partner, parents, siblings, roommates, and our pets. Social relationships include friends and acquaintances.

Community includes relationships with neighbors and members of the community and those involved in community-oriented activities. Groups, clubs, and organizations may include social clubs as well as professional, fraternal, and philanthropic groups and organizations to which you belong. Some of these may overlap into the professional category.

Career

The Career Arena includes all things pertaining to your job, career, or profession. Some professional clubs, groups, and organizations may be more appropriate in the Career Arena than in

Relationships. The career arena relates directly to your knowledge, skills, and performance on the professional front along with your degrees, titles, and licenses. Career Arena includes aspirations for promotion, advancement, recognition, and compensation, along with ownership, such as a company, store, or service outlet.

Financial

The Financial Arena includes savings, investments, and retirement issues. Include what it takes to make you feel totally and completely financially secure. List the educational needs of your children. Include material possessions you've always wanted: the cars and boats, jewels and furs, all the toys and trinkets of your dreams.

Summary

This is where you sum up your overall goals and desires. While it incorporates the basic components of the six categories with your philosophy and outlook on life, it is very general in nature.

Balance Essential

Balance is key in drafting your new life script. Skeptics may scoff, saying, "All I need is a million bucks and everything will be totally okay." Or,

"I'm fine as I am, but I'd be better if I had a perfect body." Or, "A close, personal relationship is all I ask for. Then I'll be completely happy."

Wrong! These lack blance. When you relentlessly pursue career and money—to the detriment of your home and family life—do you really think you'll be happy? There are thousands of "successful" men and women who agree, "It's lonely at the top."

Peggy Lee is famous for her poignant song *"Is That All There Is?"* Don't let lack of balance make this your theme song. Obsession with money and position leads to imbalance. You can push yourself in pursuit of goals in one arena and succeed only to find your victory is shallow because of what you've sacrificed in another arena. Think of what a bittersweet victory it would be if you achieved a goal but lost your health in the process.

Perhaps you've heard the story of John D. Rockefeller, one of the richest men in the world in his day, who could not eat or enjoy a normal meal due to stomach problems and other physical ailments brought on by his ambitious striving for his particular goals. He may have achieved wealth, but he neglected his health in the process.

There is no need to sacrifice any arena in order to have it all. Nowhere is it written that you can only get some of life's goodies at the expense of others. Balance in all areas of life is the way to achieve true, lasting health, happiness, prosperity, and peace of mind.

Are you excited? You should be, because you are about to undertake the most exciting adventure of your life. Soon you will rewrite your life script exactly the way you want it to read to create the future you really desire. You are in charge every step of the way. What you say to yourself is what you will get!

10

Create Your Future
Script It!

Now comes the exciting part—scripting your Personal Power Plan. Get seven sheets of blank paper. Put the name of an arena at the top of each one of the sheets. Again, the arena names are Mental, Physical, Spiritual, Relationships, Career, Financial, and Summary.

Start with your sheet titled: Mental. List the following sub-arenas: Educa-
Scripting your future is exciting. tion, Reading and Writing, Planning, Thinking and Studying, and Self-improvement. Leave sufficient space between to add your written script. The sub-arenas are suggestions. Substitute alternative sub-arenas that better fit your situation.

Just Start

It is important to put your thoughts down on paper to "kick-start" your creative juices. Take the word "creative" literally, because the final outcome of this exercise is the creation of your future—your new life.

Just start writing, using the sub-arenas under Mental as a guide. Describe things the way you want them to be in your intellectual life. Don't worry about how it sounds or about sentence structure. This script is yours and yours alone; you're not being graded.

For example, under Education I wrote:

"I enjoy taking courses and learning new things."
"I enroll in a new course each semester."

Under Reading and writing, I wrote:

"Reading to expand my knowledge and develop new skills excites me."

"Learning languages comes easily to me. I am becoming fluent enough to communicate with a native speaker."

Some of the sentences or phrases may seem stilted, phony, or uncomfortable. I am being very general, where you should be specific. For example, if you are planning a trip to France next year, about learning French you might write, "Learning French is

You are creating your future— your new life.

easy for me. By next March I will be able to speak French well enough to communicate with a native French speaker.'"

Continue on with Reading and Writing if they play a part in your Mental Program. You may put down something like:

"I read at least one new book each month."
My writing skills improve daily."

Take Your Time

It can take a while for you to conceive and compose your desires for all seven arenas. Take time. Relax into this exercise. Don't stress yourself. Write down your desires in the subtitles in each sub-arena. Set it aside and come back to it later.

If Planning, Thinking, and Study are part of your agenda for an improved mental state, write the statements that apply to you in these sub-arenas. Examples: "I plan in advance. My advance planning eliminates major errors." Or, "I think things through to their conclusion before making decisions."

Set it aside and come back to it.

If you've always been interested in or wanted to study art, music, dance, photography, or other areas, now is the time to get started. Remember, you would not have an interest in the subject if it were not right for you. For my writing, which initially was just an interest rather than my profession, I affirmed: "I enjoy putting my ideas on paper. I find time every day to write. Creative thoughts come to me constantly. Writing is easy for me." You may wish to create a similar affirmation focusing on the area of your particular study interest.

In Self-Improvement sub-arenas of Mental, you can really be creative. Here you script the new you, complete with all the improvements you envision. This is where you approach such areas as self-confidence, improved self-esteem, assertiveness, and whatever other characteristics you want to assimilate into your nature and persona. In Self-Improvement you may want to state one of my favorite affirmations: "I maintain a positive mental attitude." A powerful statement that has had fantastic results in my life is, "I am the best that I can be. I do whatever is necessary to improve myself."

Don't be limited by my subtitles and examples. This is your life and your script and you are the author, producer, and director of the final product, your future. Write it the way you want it to be, because that's the way it will be.

Physical Arena

Now move to the sheet with Physical Arena. List the sub-arenas: Health, Nutrition, Exercise, and Image and Appearance—again with enough space between for you to write in your personal

desires. You may want to write something like, ''I am in radiant good health. I always feel terrific. I am slim, fit, youthful, energetic and strong." Forget sentence structure or how you phrase it— just get your desires down on the paper.

Follow your health list of phrases or sentences with your thoughts on nutrition, as you want it to apply to you. Examples might be:

"I eat a well-balanced diet."

"I enjoy fruits, vegetables, dairy products, and other nutritious foods."

"I maintain my ideal weight."

Exercise

Write down your Exercise desires. Examples: "I ride my exercycle—or use my trampoline—thirty minutes each day." "I enjoy working out at the gym or I walk at least two miles every other day."

Working out at a gym may be out of the question for you, but walking may fit into your lifestyle and schedule. Your script is personal. Write down on your sheet what you want, like and, perhaps, need to do in the way of exercise.

Now let's address Image and Appearance, which is important to all of us and, again, very personal. For example, on my sheet I wrote: "l am youthful, fit, vivacious, and attractive. I am well-groomed and dress attractively. My hair and make-up are complementary. I take good care of my face and body."

Some of my sample phrases might fit you also. If so, include them. Add others. For example, if weight is an issue for you, address it here, as well as under sub-arena of Nutrition. In which sub-arena you place it, is less important than it being somewhere in the Physical Arena. Your subconscious will act on each and every statement and affirmation, regardless where you place it.

This script ultimately will become your true life story, your future.

Are you beginning to get the idea of how to draft the script for your Personal Power Plan? It's really very simple, but don't let the simplicity of this exercise fool you. This script ultimately will become your true life story, your future.

Spiritual

Move on to the next arena, Spiritual. Here you define your personal philosophy, This may seem difficult at first, especially if you haven't devoted a great deal of thought to it. Don't be intimidated. Begin with simple words and phrases that describe the inner belief system of the person you want to become. "I am an honorable person." "I look for the good in everyone I meet." "I treat others with the consideration I want to received."

You may want to be more specific than these examples in stating your personal values and belief. These examples are just to help you get started. If affiliation with a church or group is important to you, you might write, "I attend church regularly. I am an active member of the congregation." Or, if you don't maintain a formal affiliation, you might say, "My personal relationship with a higher power sustains me." "I take time everyday to pray and meditate."

Remember, your script is yours alone. It's personal and private. There is no need to worry about what others might think or feel about it No one need see, read, or hear your personal statements. You do not need the approval of anyone but yourself in preparing this script. So, be honest and true to yourself, your beliefs, and your desires for a better life when you draft this important document.

Relationships

Continue now with Relationships. If you live within a traditional family of spouse and children, you may want to address these primary relationships first.

Affirmative statements that may apply include: "I am a loving caring parent to my children." "I am a loving, caring spouse." Or, it may be "I am a loving, caring partner." Some general relationship affirmations for all living-together arrangements might be: "I am thoughtful, considerate, and giving." "I express love to those close to me." "I am a good listener."

Similar statements likely apply to social community relationships. Others may be, "I am a good friend and neighbor." "I treat my neighbors the way I want to be treated." "I am a dependable, responsible member of my organization (fill in the name)." "I am considerate, tolerant, and nonjudgmental of fellow members."

You may want to be specific in affirming in what you do for family and friends. "I call or stop in to see my parents twice a month." "I take care of the kids one afternoon a week so my partner can have some free time." "I take Mrs. Jones to the grocery store when she needs a ride."

Career

Let's move along to the Career Arena of your life. If you don't have what you consider a formal "job", don't feel left out. This category applies to all of us because we all have something we do with the major portion of our day, whether it's going to the office, maintaining a household, or pursuing a time-consuming hobby.

Here you script your job/career-oriented future the way you want it to be. Some of the statements you've already written under the Mental category might also apply here, such as those pertaining to education.

It doesn't matter which category contains the statement concerning your desires and aspirations; just be sure it's included in one or the other. As before, list the Career sub-arenas: Job-oriented skills, Degrees, Titles and Licenses, Promotion and Advancement, Recognition, and Business ownership.

Examples:

"I can type 120 words per minute without error."

"I address large groups of people with total self-confidence."

"I am a master chef."

Follow with the Degrees, Titles, and Licenses:

"I am proud of my degree."

"I am a licensed broadcast engineer."

"I can pass the California Bar the first time."

Look ahead to Promotion, Advancement, and Recognition:

"I am Employee of the Year."

"My bonus for outstanding achievement is $10,000."

"My sales exceed $380,000 this year."

"I am the region's top producer."

If being a business owner is in your future, state that exactly the way you envision it.

"I enjoy being my own boss. My employees are knowledgeable, dedicated, and productive. Our services are needed in this community.
"My company break sales records."

If you are a homemaker, be proud of it. State affirmations that make your heart sing.

"My home is a warm and friendly place."

"My family and friends compliment me constantly on my homemaking abilities."

"I am proud of my beautiful children who are bright, polite, and well-behaved."

Volunteer work of all kinds falls into this category and can be as involved and time-consuming as any career. If you volunteer, be sure to state your affirmations on this sheet.

"I am a dependable member of the team."

"I can always be relied upon to follow through on every phase I undertake."

"I am proud of my fund-raising abilities My efforts enabled our group to meet its goal."

Financial

Here you state your Financial and Investments and Retirement Needs. Again, list the sub-arenas according to your needs. Suggestions include an educational fund for your children, long term care insurance, and your other monetary requirements. Be sure to include everything necessary for you to feel completely financially secure. By now, you should have an idea how to affirm exactly what it is you desire for yourself and your family. Here are two of my personal affirmations that basically cover finances for me.

"I am accumulating a substantial estate and net worth."

"I am relaxed, comfortable, and at peace knowing that my financial affairs are in order and that I will always be financially secure."

Material Possessions

Perhaps you've been tantalized with the promise of cars, yachts, jewels, luxurious trinkets and other expensive toys, if so, include them in your want list. Do it right now. List each desired item, then write an affirmation incorporating that item, such as "I enjoy zipping around town in my red Mercedes convertible, with the top down."

"I feel truly elegant when I wear my luxurious cashmere coat."

"Looking at my gold Rolex gives me a feeling of confidence."

"I feel loved and indulged when I look at my diamond solitaire."

Summary

This is where you write general affirmations that summarize your overall Personal Power Plan. Often there may be attitudes and states of mind that seemed to have fallen through the cracks and, because they were important to me, I could not let that happen. These are overall affirmations that are imperative to my well-being. Perhaps some will be meaningful for you and you'll want to include them on your PPP.

"I am happy". Seeking happiness is universal. We want to be happy in our relationships and home life and career. Being healthy and financially secure would surely make us happier. Fulfilling our wishes in every category would add to our happiness. Therefore, being happy could be considered an overall desire or a summary of

many desires. If you resonate with this, you may want to affirm "I am happy!" on your Summary sheet.

Another powerful overall affirmation is "I have peace of mind." Being happy and having peace of mind go hand in hand. You'd be amazed

at the positive effects of these two simple pro-
nouncements. Another excellent summarizing
statement to add to your sheet is the classic formula by the renowned French psychotherapist
Emile Coue, "Everyday in every way I am getting
better and better."

A comforting summary statement I often turn
to is, "I am fully equipped for the divine plan for
my life." Another powerful summary statement
is, "I am in possession of my goals. My subconscious mind will lead me in their manifestation."
This summary enables me to be patient, knowing
that I am making progress.

"I do whatever is necessary to achieve my
goals." When you have affirmed "I do whatever
is necessary" to the point that your subconscious
accepts that statement as fact, you will do whatever is necessary to improve yourself, to achieve
your goals, or to do whatever completes the "I do
whatever is necessary" statement.

Obviously, I hope you will not carry doing
whatever is necessary to inappropriate lengths
that may include illegal or immoral acts, or to en-
gage in actions that might cause harm of any sort
to you or anyone or anything. You may consider
this a silly warning. However, I strongly feel it
to be a legitimate and necessary. We are working
with powerful forces; we are programming our
subconscious mind. What we say is what we get.
You will, in fact, find yourself doing whatever

is necessary, and that can be wonderfully constructive, as long as you work exclusively toward
positive results.

Incorporate a Conditioner

The way to circumvent negative effects is to incorporate a conditioner into your affirmation—or
at least into your mind-set as you affirm. There
are three phrases that will suffice, depending
upon the wording of your affirmation. Add the
one that seems most appropriate to your affirmation. Alternatively, if you tend to get hung up on
wording, you can place the conditioner phrase
at the end of all your affirmations, thus covering
everything,

The three phrases follow. The important words
are those within quotes. These words in parenthe-
ses are simply my suggested lead-ins to the very
important conditioner phrase.

I ask for "the highest good of all concerned."
When you ask that you receive or achieve something and you consider the highest good of all
concerned, no one will be hurt or deprived because of your receiving or achieving.

I ask for "this, or its equivalent" or "this, or
something better." This is an unequaled phrase to
use when asking for something. It assures that if
you do not get exactly what you ask for, you will
at least get its equivalent or something better.

I give thanks that what I ask for comes to me "under grace in a perfect way." This statement assures you that when you get what you ask for, it doesn't have any negative side effects. For example, if you ask for a certain sum of money, you don't want it to come to you as an insurance payment for an injury or the settlement of an ugly legal matter. You want it to come to you under grace in a perfect way.

A Rough Draft

That's it for now. You have your rough draft of your Personal Power Plan. In the next chapter, we'll discuss the proper wording of your affirmations for maximum effectiveness. It is essential that they be worded properly. And, we'll give you a few key phrases that will accelerate and assure the manifestation process.

11

Affirm Your Script
First Person Positive

Now that you have a rough draft of your Personal Power Plan scripted, you want to be sure you have your affirmations are worded for maximum effectiveness. You certainly don't want to sabotage your PPP by inadvertently using improper or ineffectual wording.

Use The Present Tense

The present tense is "I am," not "I will," "I'm going to," "I expect to," or "I'll try." Only "I am" is in the present tense; it states what is. The other statements are in the future tense and are vague, as in the case of "I expect to" or "I'm going to." "I'll try" is a useless phrase and if you ever catch yourself saying it, determine here and now to eliminate it from your vocabulary. Just what does try mean? In this context it means to make an attempt. Is that wishy-washy or what? Your affirmations are a declaration of what is, not a weak attempt at trying. You either mean what you affirm or you don't; trying doesn't count.

State As An Actuality

You must state your affirmation as if your statement were an actual fact, not a wished for or hoped for dream. Your subconscious, that never-questioning, obedient servant of yours, will work to make your statement a reality. For years, it's been acting on your negative input; now, properly programmed, it will do what is necessary to bring goals, needs, and desires into manifestation.

Be Definite, Not Vague

Vague goals bring vague results. Definite goals bring definite results. You're constructing your wish list, your letter to Santa, your request of the genie in the bottle. Seriously, this is your request of the universe. What you say—that is, what you state in your affirmations—is what you get. You must be clear, concise, exact.

When you buy a pair of shoes, you state the exact size. When you buy a shirt, you state the exact size. If you didn't, the shoes or the shirt would not fit. In this instance, you must be certain the

affirmation you state fits your personal, individual need or it will not fit your circumstance.

Express Gratitude

This goes back to our formula. Of course you should be grateful, appreciative, and thankful for the manifestation of your desires. Be so! And, be so in advance. Be grateful, appreciative, and thankful when you state your affirmation as if the statement were indeed a fact. It already is a fact in another dimension, it just hasn't materialized yet. A sincere feeling of gratitude helps to speed things up.

Experience Expected Feelings

This is vitally important. Your thoughts and your personal statements elicit feelings. Your feelings determine reality in your emotional state before they manifest physically or materially. If you repeatedly think and say to yourself, "Life is rotten, everything's going straight down the tubes." How do you feel? You feel rotten and as if everything's going down the tubes, right? Pretty soon, what is the result? Life becomes rotten and everything starts going down the tubes.

Emotions Impact

Have you ever blushed? Your feelings of embarrassment make your skin flush. Have you ever had sweaty palms? Your feelings make your palms damp. Have you ever had cold or hot sweats at night due to worry or a bad dream? Your feelings caused the change in your body temperature. Do you cry on occasion? Your feelings cause the tears. Feelings are extremely powerful. Consider these visible manifestations of feelings and then consider the invisible manifestations within your body that other strong feelings can create.

Feelings are extremely powerful.

Perhaps your thoughts, which cause your feelings, if unchecked, can cause breakdowns in the bodily mechanism thereby creating illness and disease. Given this possibility, it becomes even more essential to control wayward thoughts and feelings. By the same token, happy and peaceful thoughts and their subsequent feelings are to be encouraged. They have a healing, therapeutic effect on the body and thus promote good health and contentment. Through your personal script and affirmations, you have the ability to properly direct your thoughts.

Let me give you a few examples that demonstrate various ways of wording your affirmations for optimum results. Let's take one of the most popular and universal goals in the world: to lose weight. Perhaps that's one of the goals, or affirmations, you placed on your Physical list. You've jotted down, "Want (or need) to lose weight." Now let's look at some wrong ways, and then some right ways to word this affirmation. Wrong: "I hope to lose weight one of these days." That's stated in the future tense. Remember, affirmations must be stated in the present tense. Also, "hope" is vague; "will" would have been better. Wrong: "My goal is to lose some weight." "Some weight" is vague. How much weight do you want to lose? Right: "I weigh 125 pounds."

This is stated in the present tense as if your weight goal has already been achieved, and 125 pounds is a definite figure for your subconscious to work toward. In this case, be reasonable. If 125 pounds is not appropriate for your basic body type, don't confuse your subconscious. You don't want to become emaciated in your attempt to be slim. You might like to add, "I enjoy feeling slim and comfortable in my clothes." This demonstrates the feelings you'll have when you achieve the weight stated in your affirmation. And, when you say it, let your gratitude be apparent in your voice as you record, and in your thoughts as you listen to, your tape.

Next to losing weight, or maybe right up there with it, is the desire to stop smoking. If that's one of your Physical/ Health goals, perhaps you've written, "Try to stop smoking" As I mentioned, to try is "to make an attempt at". Trying or making an attempt at not smoking will not make you smoke-free. You either smoke or you don't smoke; trying not to smoke will not stop you from smoking. To stop smoking, do not smoke, period.

Here are some right and wrong ways to word your stop smoking affirmations. Wrong: "I'm going to try to stop smoking." Notice the future tense in the phrase going to. Try, as we know, is to make an attempt at, which never works. If I'm sounding repetitive here, remember that repetition is what gets the job done and I want you to be doing, not trying. Right: "I don't smoke." You could also say, "I no longer smoke," but I think plain "I don't smoke" is stronger. If you say, "I no longer smoke," you're constantly reminding yourself that you used to smoke and that may be a negative. However, if you're extremely proud of yourself because you no longer smoke, that may

Having money is a universal desire. be the better affirmation for you because it evokes the feeling of pride in having given up an unwanted habit. Also, if you firmly state, "I don't smoke," when cigarettes are offered to you, that statement will be accepted. If you say "I'm trying to quit smoking," like as not you'll hear, "Oh come on. One more won't hurt!" These affirmative statements are also easily adapted to other major concerns, such as eliminating alcohol from your life. You may want to reinforce your "I don't smoke" or "I no longer smoke" affirmation with something like the following: "I enjoy breathing fresh air." "My lungs are healthy and strong." "I am smoke-free; now my food has far more taste."

The terms, goals, affirmations, needs, and desires are often interchangeable. Another universal desire is to have more money. Or, perhaps your desire for more money is expressed as more sales. Both of the foregoing could be placed under Career, or the need or desire for money in a general way could be under Financial. Please don't get hung up about the category in which you place your desire, just get it in there somewhere.

Wrong: "My goal is to make more money or more sales." This is vague. How much more money? And how do you measure more sales? When do you expect to make more money or to increase your sales?

Right: "I am the top biller in the company."
Present tense. "I am pleased and grateful that my
sales gross is over $350,000 per year." This state-
ment presents a definite figure to be achieved,
and it expresses pleasure and a feeling of gratitude. One of my favorite overall financial goals is,
"I have sufficient funds to maintain a very good
standard of living, to enjoy total comfort, and to
provide for all of my desires." While a specific
dollar figure is not mentioned, the entire statement is definite in that my funds must be sufficient to cover my standard of living total comfort,
and all of my desires.

Another good overall statement is, "Money
continually comes to me under grace in perfect
ways." This powerful affirmation utilizes the
important conditioner mentioned in the previous
chapter. The "under grace and in perfect ways"
phrase assures that the money that continues
to come in is not as a result of a situation that is
undesirable, such as receiving undeserved payments for welfare, unemployment compensation,
or a disability, or monies earned illegally or under
a cloud of anger and resentment such as from an
acrimonious divorce settlement mat has harmed
your children.

Here's an affirmation that might be on your
Mental list: "Read more books." Wrong: "I want
to get more reading done." That's vague, in the
future tense. When and how much more reading

do you want to get done? Right: "I read a new book each month." That's in the present tense and it's definitive. You state that you read a new book each month. Right: "I easily find time in each day to read books that help me advance in my career." Present tense again. "Easily" denotes a feeling. The "advance in my career" can be a feeling as well as an incentive. You may want to add even more feeling to your reading statement by adding, as it applies, "Reading relaxes me. My work stress melts away with each page I turn."

I live in the Oakland hills and, after the huge fire that destroyed 1000s of homes, my first priority was to replace my very old and dry shake roof with a fireproof or fire resistant roof. Pete put a new roof on my son's home in Santa Rosa to my son's total satisfaction, so I decided to hire Pete for my roof job. Because Pete is also from Santa Rosa, over sixty miles away, it was decided he would bunk in his sleeping bag in my living room during the project in order to avoid a twice-daily long commute. This turned out to be a great experience for me because Pete, to my total surprise, turned out to be one of the most spiritual people I've ever met. He says, because he works on roofs, he's a little closer to heaven than the rest of us. We had many interesting conversations at the end of each workday about a variety of subjects including truth, understanding, and enlightenment. Pete is really into tapes as I am, and he regularly attends talks, seminars, workshops, and retreats on related subjects. Pete expressed the desire to find enlightenment and gain understanding. He phrased his desires in question form: "How can I find enlightenment and understanding? When will I know the truth?" Affirmations cannot be stated in question form because questions do not fit the rules stated at the beginning of this chapter. The following spiritual affirmations illustrate how I worded these desires.

"I thirst for knowledge and constantly search for truth, understanding, and enlightenment through books, tapes, and other means."

"I enjoy contemplating the spiritual and metaphysical, and new understanding comes to me everyday."

"I spend time in philosophical thought and meditation each and every day."

One of the strongest desires in the world is to find a mate. Obviously, this belongs in the Relationships category. My friend Theresa was searching for Mr. Wonderful. She put out the affirmation "Many new men now enter my life." It worked. Many indicates quantity, and that's what she got, lots of men. But that turned out to be a wrong affirmation for her because the men who entered her life were not appropriate for her. She was not specific. Here are better ways to word her Mr. Wonderful affirmation. Right: "The man I am now attracting into my life is single, successful, and financially secure." This eliminated the married, unsuccessful deadbeats that previously came to her in droves. "He is able to take care of me materially and emotionally." This was important to Theresa. And, because she has children from her first marriage, this was also important: "He is kind and generous to me and my children."

My friend, Hans, is a marathon runner. Running figures predominantly in more than one of his categories. Obviously running is physical. And, because he retired after many years in civil service, running has become his retirement career. It's his hobby; it's what he does. Here are some ways of wording his marathon and other running affirmations. Wrong: "My goal is to run a faster marathon." That's vague. How much faster? Right: "My goal in running is to beat my personal best of [time]." That's definite. "I run a [time] marathon easily, without effort" That's present tense, states a definite time, and expresses desired feelings, "easily and without effort." Another, and this is not for the faint-hearted: "I am running across America this year." Yes, you read that right. Hans is running across America as I write. This four-month run through fifteen states from New York to San Francisco has been his major goal since he began running. Hans has repeated that "I am running across America this year" to

RUNNING ACROSS AMERICA

himself and others dozens of times. This statement has now become a reality for him.

Why would Hans want to take on such a grueling experience? He says, "As a German immigrant who came to America, I wish to express my appreciation for the good life and many opportunities afforded me. My run across America seems to be the most visible way to accomplish this. I am a public speaker and marathon runner recently retired after 35 years of federal government service. This country has been very good to me and I want to give back.

Hans plans to speak to schools, community groups, and civic organization along the way to raise consciousness of the American public to the plight of children in need. He wants to challenge and encourage organizations and individuals to whom he speaks to become involved in order to help improve certain poor conditions facing youth.

All of these feelings and emotions are tied up in Hans' statement, "I am running across America this year." When he says it, he experiences pride, gratitude, and the feeling of contribution to the betterment of society. It has always been an "I am" not an "I'm going to" thing with Hans and his statement is definite and not vague.

These examples are provided to give you an idea about how to construct your own personal affirmations. Just think present tense, not future; act as if your affirmation were already a fact; be definite, not vague; state your affirmations with a feeling of gratitude in your heart; and, while stating and listening to your affirmations, elicit the feelings you expect to have when the manifestation occurs.

12

Record It

Power of the Spoken Word

Of our five senses, hearing is considered by many to be the most important. It has been proven that babies sense sounds while still in the womb. Babies are attuned to their mother's heartbeat and breathing. Some expectant parents sing and read to their unborn in the belief that the fetus hears and gains comfort from the sounds of its parents' voices. Yes, sound—or hearing—is our primary sense. Infants and grown people alike react to familiar sounds and voices. This basic fact has been taken into consideration in the overall design and long-term effectiveness of your Personal Power Plan.

Your PPP is developed around the use of thoughts and words—your thoughts and your words—that will be recorded by a familiar voice, preferably yours, and that will then become familiar sounds. You will react to these familiar sounds in the same positive way the newborn reacts to the sounds it remembers from when in mother's womb.

The Bible says God created the universe with first His thought and then His word. I believe that we are made in our creator's image because we have within us similar divine God-given cre-

ative abilities. We have the ability to think, we have the ability to make choices about what we think, and we have the ability to create our individual worlds through the personal expression of our thoughts through our words. We were born with the ability and the privilege through thought, choice, and words, to create our own perfect personal world and universe. This is our

Your words are the backbone of your Personal Power Plan.

divine right, privilege, and obligation. If we ignore this—if we do not do everything within our abilities to create our perfect lives full of health, happiness, and abundance, we are not living up to our divine potential. Your PPP is designed to help you achieve the divine potential that is rightfully yours while enjoying your personally designed world of health, happiness, and abundance, which is also rightfully yours.

You have already exercised your freedom of choice in putting your thoughts concerning your personal goals, desires, and aspirations down on paper. You have phrased your thoughts in words that are meaningful to you. Now it is time to think about recording those words in a familiar voice so that the end result—the words—will have the greatest impact possible on your subconscious and cause whatever you have chosen to happen.

I am in love with and excited about words. As a reader, I delight in various writers' styles. I honestly enjoy reading Roget's *Thesaurus* for its synonyms and to gain a new light on my favorite words, and my worn copy has been my constant companion on every desk I've ever occupied. As a writer of radio commercials, I wanted to fight to the death anyone who would suggest cutting one of my perfectly chosen words for the sake of brevity. There are only so many words that can fit in a twenty, thirty, or sixty second radio commercial and, if I put one in for a reason, it was meant to stay.

As a listener, I'm equally fascinated with the words I hear when listening to the radio, television, a tape, or a live speaker. As someone who has spoken into a microphone for a good portion of my career, I am aware of the amazing power of the spoken word. As a writer, I understand that it is my compulsion to put my thoughts and ideas on paper that motivates and drives me.

Your Personal Words Are Important

The words you have so carefully chosen are vitally important. They are the backbone of your PPP. Of equal importance is the voice that expresses your words on the tape that you will create. Think about the many familiar voices that play a part in your life. There are the voices of the various members of your family and of your friends, teachers, coworkers, and business associates. But what about the other voices? The invisible voices? I'm talking about radio voices in particular for a number of reasons. You may not realize it, but radio voices have an insidious way of working themselves into your memory bank.

I was brought up on radio because there was no TV when I was a child. In my grandmother's house there was a room that we called the radio room. Today, it would be a TV room, of course. There we sat, as a family, but we were really alone with our thoughts. As we listened, we visualized the drama that was unfolding through our ears and sense of hearing. You see, the picture was in our minds rather than on the TV screen. I like to call listening without a picture or something to

watch tuning into the theater of the mind. The theater of the mind is far superior to any theatrical or television production. My theater of the mind productions may be totally different from yours, but that is fine. Mine are magnificent, and I am very happy with them.

This same phenomenon goes into effect when you read a novel that is later made into a movie. How many times have you been disappointed with the screen version, and said that the movie wasn't nearly as good as the book? That's because, when reading, your personal theater of the mind goes into production and you mentally visualize the characters, locations, and action. Then, when you see the movie, it doesn't compare with your own production, and you're disappointed.

Many of the old-time radio dramas still bring up very powerful mental images for me today as I reminisce about favorite programs of long ago. Do you recall "The Lone Ranger"? How about "The Whistler," "Inner Sanctum," "The Shadow," and "Dragnet"? My theater of the mind worked overtime during those dramas! Less dramatic but still impressive to me were programs such as the "Jack Benny Show," "The Chase & Sanborn Hour," and "The Hit Parade." Nightly at the dinner table, back home in New Jersey during the thirties and forties, our family listened to "Easy Aces," a husband and wife comedy team, followed by Lowell Thomas and the news. Many years later it was a thrill for me to see Mr. Thomas when he addressed the National Association of Broadcasters and hear him say, in person, his famous closing line that I'd heard hundreds of times: "So long until tomorrow."

Stan Freeberg is another name whose voice is familiar to radio buffs. He did a classic piece several years ago entitled "Anybody Here Remember Radio?" In the piece he was lamenting the fact that there aren't any radio programs on the air these days. A ten-year-old girl in the audience questioned him, saying, "What's a radio program?" When he described some of the programs of the olden days—the forties—that had actors, live musicians, sound effects men, and guest stars, she said, "Oh, you mean like a television program when the picture tube blows out!" Then she asked, "What did you look at?" Freeberg replied, "You didn't look at anything, you just listened." "Boy," the girl says, "talk about your radical ideas!" Freeberg explained that you had to use your imagination and, with the help of sound effects, he proceeded to give a demonstration. What followed in the next two minutes is, in my opinion, the best argument ever in favor of the power of imagination and the theater of the mind and one of the funniest bits I have ever heard. Please note the word heard.

In the demonstration, Freeberg said, "OK people, now when I give you the cue, I want the

five-hundred-foot mountain of whipped cream
to be shoved into Lake Michigan, which has been
drained and filled with hot chocolate. Then the
Royal Canadian Air Force
will appear overhead

*Radio stretches
the imagination.*

towing a tendon mara-
schino cherry, which will
be dropped into the whipped cream to the cheering of 25,000 extras. All right! Cue the mountain.
[Sound of a 500-foot mountain of whipped cream
being shoved into Lake Michigan.] Cue the Air
Force. [Sound of a squadron of planes flying
overhead.] Cue the maraschino cherry. [Sound of
a 500-pound cherry dropping into the whipped
cream.] OK, 25,000 cheering extras. [Sound of
25,000 cheering extras.] Now, do you want to try
that on television?" asked Freeberg sarcastically.

"I see what you mean, " replied the girl, convinced. "You see," Freeberg continued, "radio
was a very special medium because it stretched
the imagination." "Doesn't television stretch the
imagination?" asked the girl. "Up to twenty-one
inches, yes," Freeberg commented dryly. You're
probably wondering why on earth I find this so
funny. The reason is that I heard it whereas here
you only read it. Therein lies the big difference.
When I listen to this on tape, my imagination
goes into gear. I am fully present in the theater of
the mind. I can picture the mountain of whipped
cream being shoved into Lake Michigan. The hot

chocolate is so real I can almost taste it. I can see and hear the Royal Canadian Air Force as they fly over the site towing a ten-ton maraschino cherry. The sound of the cherry dropping into the whipped cream is magnificent, as is my mental image of the splash. And the 25,000 cheering extras are real people with faces that I can recognize. I can appreciate doing something like this on radio with a low budget because I've written and produced commercials with similar elaborate sound effects at very little cost. Can you imagine the problems involved, to say nothing of the cost, of trying to produce that Freeberg scenario for TV?

Words Stretch Imagination

The point is that what you hear does stretch the imagination, in addition to impressing the subconscious, in ways that other senses do not. It is said that a picture is worth a thousand words. In some cases that may be true if you see or look at the picture. If you don't see the picture it's absolutely worthless. This is one of the biggest obstacles I routinely met when selling air time, especially when the competition was newspaper or any form of print advertising. Potential advertisers were hooked on pictures. They'd cut out their expensive newspaper ads and tack them on the wall over their desk. Some would even frame them. "See, there's my ad. What have I got to show for my money after a radio spot airs?"

First of all, it's unlikely his hoped-for customer cares enough about his ad to frame it or tack it to his wall in order to keep it in front of his nose. Secondly—and this is the important part—while a print message can be retained in such a manner, a verbal message, whether consciously listened to or not, is permanently retained in the subconscious. The spoken word slips into our subconscious even if we're not actively listening.

Let's get back to voices again, familiar voices are believable voices. And, let's refer to radio again in doing so. As a creature of habit, before I got hooked on tapes, I listened to the radio daily. I listened in the morning while I was getting ready to go to work. I listened to my car radio on the way to the station and again on the way home. While I did not always listen to my station while at home or when commuting, I listened to the station for which I worked all day when in my office, because what was being broadcast on our air was piped into every office. Yes, we were the basic captive audience; we listened. And at night I listened even more as

A verbal message, whether consciously listened to or not, is permanently retained in the subconscious.

I watched and listened to television. The upshot was that the voices I listened to, or heard, soon became familiar voices and, with few exceptions, believable voices. Why is this important?

Because, for the most part, the voice on the radio is asking or telling you to do something, to buy something, to call some business or service, or to go somewhere. Some action is usually requested. Because over time the voice has become familiar and believable, eventually you act on the voice's request or demand. That's what radio advertising is all about. It's designed to get action. If it didn't work, advertisers would not spend the huge amounts they do on radio and TV advertising.

Familiar Voices

Sometimes you'll hear a very familiar voice, such as a famous movie star, doing a television voice-over. A voice-over is exactly what it implies; it's a voice that is heard over the pictured commercial. One such commercial that sticks in my mind is for a well-known soup company with Jimmy Stewart doing the voice-over. His voice is distinctive, so it's familiar, I don't need to see his face to know it's Jimmy Stewart. And because he's believable and trustworthy, I get the warm fuzzies when he tells how

A believable voice told me to buy that brand of soup.

soothing and nourishing a hot cup of that soup is on a cold winter's evening. His telling me about the wonderful properties of this soup is like a personal reference.

So when I go to the grocery store and come to the soup aisle, guess which brand of soup I put in my cart? I pick Jimmy's soup because I've heard of it from someone familiar. A believable voice told me to buy that brand of soup. I may look at other unknown or unadvertised brands, but I probably won't pick them because I never heard of them. I may not realize it but, subliminally, I'm being manipulated by an invisible yet familiar, believable voice in my head.

Maybe you feel you don't respond in the intended way to famous voices such as Jimmy Stewart's or any of the other invisible voices I've mentioned. Nevertheless, I'd wager that on occasion when discussing the merits of a particular brand, service, or place of business, you've said, "I've never heard of that," basically dismissing its credibility. On the other hand, your having heard of a particular brand or business gives it a greater chance of acceptance and, therefore, your business. The more this is reinforced through repetition, the more apt you are to act on the voice's message, request, or demand.

Whose voice is most familiar to you? Whose voice is most believable? Of all the invisible voices in your mind, whose is most persistent? The answer is yours! Yours is the voice on the mental tape in your head that we spoke about earlier—the one that never stops, the relentless nag that both chides and encourages, ridicules and congratulates, fumes and soothes. Now is the time to put this dynamic force to work for you in a positive manner.

Record Your Personal Power Plan

Yes, now is the time to personally record your Personal Power Plan script. I encourage you to do just that, to personally record this life-changing document. If you do so, it will be far more effective than if your PPP were recorded by anyone else. One obvious reason is that you must believe the message in order to achieve the results. If you can't believe yourself, who can you believe?

Secondly, your PPP script is a private document that you may prefer to keep confidential. Unless you're terribly nervous about taping, there's no reason to introduce another party into

Find a quiet place to record where you won't be disturbed. this very special, intimate, and personal matter, your personal transformation process. Taping your PPP script is easy. All you need is an inexpensive portable audio recorder.

To record, you'll want to find a quiet place where you won't be interrupted during the time you're taping. Put the recorder on a desk or table, rather than your lap, for stability. My desk is a big old metal office desk, which I really like because of its size and drawer capacity. It has metal pull-outs over the drawers and last time I taped, I put my recorder on one of these pull-outs.

Hold your script in any way that feels comfortable. If you've never recorded before, you'll want to play around with the recorder until you get the hang of it. Do the "testing—one, two, three, four—testing" bit until you feel comfortable with the controls and your voice. It's normal to be surprised at the sound of your own voice the first time you hear yourself on tape. "Is that me?" is the usual reaction. The beauty of audio recording is that all mistakes can be corrected so you need not be concerned about voice, diction, or delivery. If you blow it, simply stop, rewind until the flub is eliminated, and resume recording. This assurance is very comforting. I remember my early TV years in the fifties and early sixties, before the advent of videotape, when all programming was live. All of my mistakes, gaffes, faux pas, and blunders went out live for all the world to see. I would have loved to have a rewind button back then to eliminate those embarrassing moments.

Don't worry about your voice or delivery. The recording is for you and you alone. The important thing is getting the message recorded so you can listen to it repeatedly. Even if you think you sound like you're speaking from the bottom of a barrel, don't worry about it. The words are what count. If you feel the quality is really bad, you might want to try recording your message in a smaller room with less background noise as there might be in a larger room.

Experiment to get the best quality you possibly can so you won't feel compelled to rerecord your entire script after you've finished recording it. I recorded mine in one take in my upstairs office and it's served me well over all these years!

If you feel you simply can't handle recording your own voice, don't give up on this important project. Someone else can do it for you. I know many people with voicemail phobia who simply will not leave a message on any machine because they have a thing about being recorded. If you fall into that category, honor it. I don't want you to be intimidated or to do anything that doesn't feel right or comfortable to you. Recruit someone you trust to record your script for you. It's preferable to find someone with a familiar, believable voice: a friend, neighbor, coworker, or relative. If need be, hire someone. The most important thing is to get the words on tape so that you can listen to them over and over again.

I have recorded scripts for a few friends and relatives, and the end result for them has probably been as good as if they did the job themselves. In fact, one friend dropped me a line just this week to tell me that she still listens regularly to the tape I prepared for her two years ago. She states, "My tape has been helpful to me. Every time I play it, four days a week, I listen to my success." Her primary goals were to establish a new relationship and to advance her career. In the two-year period, several eligible new men entered her life and they keep coming. Her career has really taken off and she has opened a new successful business and, in her note, she hinted that an exciting new venture is now in the works.

You, too, can create new relationships, new business ventures, new successes in every area of your life. But you must get started now. As the sports company says, "Just do it!"

Record your script—or have it recorded—today. Here's another tip: When you're personally taping, go through the entire script—that is, all of your categories—in the first person. Example: "I am youthful, fit, vivacious, and attractive." Then, go through the entire script in the second person. Example: "You are youthful, fit, vivacious, and attractive." Finally, go through the entire script again using your first name. Example: "Alice is youthful, fit, vivacious, and attractive."

If someone is taping for you, repeat the above process except, after each first-person statement, pause for the length of the statement for you, the listener and author of the PPP script, to mentally repeat the statement or, in order to keep the entire recording within a time limit, simply repeat the words to yourself mentally while the voice is stating your affirmations. This is to avoid any confusion that may occur when another voice is saying "I" to you. If you repeat the "I" statements to yourself mentally, you will get the same impact as if you had recorded the material yourself.

Why go through the process of recording the entire script three times? For repetition. You do remember the importance of repetition, I'm sure. In addition, by hearing the message presented in three very personal ways, "I," "you," and by your first name, you are treating your subconscious mind to a triple whammy. People react strongly to each of the three approaches. One may have a greater impact than

Repetition.
Repetition.
Repetition.

another on you personally. You might as well take advantage of the three-way approach and get full benefit from each of your carefully worded affirmations.

13

Analyze It. Utilize It
Ruts and Repetition

In personal programming, the operative word is *repetition*. It is the most important action you can take to assure success in the vital undertaking of reprogramming your life.

Now that you've written your script to your individual specifications and you have recorded it as prescribed, you're ready to reap the benefits of your Personal Power Plan. From now on, it's easy—it's downhill all the way. All you have to do is practice repetition: listen repeatedly to your tape.

All you have to do is practice repetition: listen repeatedly to your tape.

Listen. Listen. Listen.

Listen at every opportunity. The more you listen, the faster the results. Don't listen haphazardly—listen at regular times throughout the day. After sufficient repetitions, the thoughts and words will be deeply embedded in your subconscious; therefore, you will automatically act on the personal statements you hear yourself repeating.

It is said that any new activity repeated consistently for twenty-one days will become a habit. Therefore, listening to your PPP at least three times each day for a minimum of twenty-one days is absolutely vital. For the following twenty-one days, I recommend listening twice daily, morning and night, preferably before retiring so your subconscious can continue to work on the message while you sleep. After the second twenty-one-day period, continue to listen at least once a day, or more often for better results. Continue listening indefinitely for maintenance.

I keep inexpensive recorders in almost every room of my house. That way, there's always one handy and it's more sensible than carrying a single recorder from room to room. I have recorders in the kitchen, living room, office, every bedroom, and my bathroom. I have an extensive library of CDs I've made and listening to one that suits my mood helps me get through boring chores. I listen while doing dishes, dusting, polishing silver, making beds, folding clothes, paying bills and, of course, putting on make-up.

I have a good quality recorder with earphones that I use on my daily personal exercise walk and my evening walk with Charlie, my feisty Spitz. This is what I also take with me when I anticipate finding myself in the interminable post office line, which I find hard to tolerate without either listening to or reading something. If you're going to buy a recorder, I suggest investing in a good product since you only need one of these versus the more-than-one inexpensive players you might care to put in various rooms as I do.

My recorder has a clip on case for attaching it to a belt. I use it with an inexpensive special belt that has a pocket for the recorder so my arms are free to swing and hands are free to hold Charlie's leash. These adjustable one-size-fits-all foam rubber belts are available in department and sporting goods stores for about ten dollars.

So, now that you've got one or more recorders on hand, let's get started. I suggest that men listen in the morning while shaving, driving to work, walking to the office or store from the parking lot or subway station, and while in line at the bank or post office. Women should listen while putting on their makeup to get their day started on a positive note, as well as when commuting and standing in various lines as do their male counterparts. Everyone should listen while driving, walking, running, riding a stationary bike, doing housework, gardening, or while doing other activities that do not require active thinking.

Please note that your PPP tape is not designed to be a meditation tape. It is not necessary to get into a hypnotic state before listening. In fact, that is to be discouraged. Being relaxed is fine, of course, but being hypnotized is not. The beauty and effectiveness

Your PPP tape is not designed to be a meditation tape. It is not necessary to get into a hypnotic state before listening.

of your PPP tape is that you are encouraged to listen to it anywhere and everywhere, except when total concentration to detail is required.

Works on Subconscious Mind

The carefully constructed, all-important message you'll be hearing will work its magical powers on your subconscious mind to program you for the future you've designed for yourself. In addition you'll be reaping other benefits. You'll be turning wasted time into productive time. What else can you do while shaving or putting on your face? You might as well program your mind beneficially.

Listening in traffic to your potent affirmations will lessen driving stress normally associated with commuting. Listening while standing in line will make those bothersome waits less frustrating and time will pass more quickly. Listening while doing routine household tasks and yard work will give you a way to utilize your mind as well as your hands. The same goes for routine exercise, which can often be so boring. Mundane tasks will become doubly productive when you combine them with listening to your PPP tape.

After sufficient repetitions, your personal message will sink into your subconscious. It will be written in concrete on your brain matter. After your subconscious really gets the message, it will act on it. That's precisely what you want. If this sounds a bit intimidating or even scary, remember that you wrote the script, and you recorded the message. These are your words, your wishes, your desires, and your goals. If there's anything you don't like about your PPP, change it now, because what you say to yourself is what you will get. Your words are the cause, the desired result is the effect. This is how the law of cause and effect will work for you.

Did you know that radio and television waves go out into the universe and keep on going forever? Every time I think about this, I really crack up. When I remember my first radio program, "Alice in Slumberland," and think about it going out into the universe ad infinitum, I have to laugh.

Perhaps there are beings on other planets listening to all of our old broadcasts, including "Alice in Slumberland." Because our thoughts have vibrations and tions and

After sufficient repetitions, your personal message will sink into your subconscious.

energy and, in many ways, are similar to radio and TV waves, they also go out into the universe. So, as you listen to your tape and think about the words being said, the vibrations are going out into the universe. This is the cause that will result in the effect you have predetermined, the manifestation of your desires and goals.

Do Whatever is Necessary

One of the affirmations I put on my personal tape states, "I do whatever is necessary to improve myself." This is a powerful statement and one not to be taken lightly. Whenever I'm dissatisfied with myself in any way, my subconscious says, "Do whatever is necessary," because it's been imprinted with that message. If it's a weight problem, I find myself automatically decreasing my food intake. If I think I look flabby, I find myself signing up for an exercise program. If I don't like my hair, which happens frequently, I find myself sitting in the chair of a new hair stylist. I gave this statement to a close friend who ended up having her teeth capped, having a tummy tuck, and an eye job. You can see that this is a powerful statement mat is not to be taken lightly.

I modified this statement to include my house. I bought my present house under stress and in a hurry. I wanted to be in a new residence for the Christmas holidays. Then, for years after, I lusted after every other house I'd looked at previously or that came up for sale in the area after my purchase, berating myself for making such an important decision hastily. I remembered all the lovely, stately homes I had looked at and turned down because each one needed some renovation and I wasn't into mess and commotion.

I was into outside living; I really wanted every room to open outside. But I found myself in a house that was more like an East Coast house than a California dwelling. There was no way to get to the backyard except through a kitchen side door and down a long alleyway.

> *I decided to adapt the "l do whatever is necessary" statement to my house.*

I realized, in hindsight, that the only reason I bought the house, in addition to the fact that I thought I only deserved a small, vine-covered cottage, was because my furniture fit into it perfectly without any additions or deletions.

Finally, I decided to adapt the "l do whatever is necessary" statement to my house. I said, "I do whatever is necessary to make my house my dream home." Soon I found myself consulting contractors, designers, and architects. Before long, I had a new kitchen under construction.

Then a few walls came out, making the interior lighter and more spacious. Next, a bold step. With great trepidation, I instructed John, my contractor, to cut through the walls of two rooms that faced the backyard and install French doors in both rooms. Cutting huge holes in the outside walls of my house provoked a massive attack of nerves. Would I be sorry? Once the gigantic saw started its job, we were beyond the point of no return.

I'm happy to report the decision to go ahead was one of the best I've ever made. Now, all my ground-level rooms open outside, from either the front, side, or back. But mess and commotion? There is nothing as impossible or more unnerving than attempting to live a civilized life in a dwelling while remodeling or renovating it. Harlan, the man who refinished my floors, told me he's personally witnessed several divorces in homes he's worked in during long-term renovating projects. Mess and commotion can bring out the worst in people.

Nevertheless, my remodeling didn't stop there. The "I do whatever is necessary to make my house my dream home" statement wouldn't leave me alone until I literally did everything possible to make the house I live in my dream home. I needed a guest room and an office. The statement was relentless: "Do whatever is necessary," it said. And so I did. There was more mess and commotion, lots more, but now I have a beautiful guest room, an extra bath, and an office.

Now, as I look at my yard and garden after a bit of neglect over this rainy holiday season, I wonder if I should say, "I do whatever is necessary to have a beautiful garden." Perhaps I will. But I know it is a powerful statement and not one to be taken lightly.

Because I'm writing this as one year ends and a new one begins, I'm reminded of the changes that each new year brings; changes that must be made and changes that we wish to make. This is a human characteristic and why people worldwide make New Year's resolutions. Yearly we resolve to do better, be better. One way to do and be better is to get out of our ruts, as comfortable and fur-lined as they may be.

Ruts

What is a rut? Webster defines a rut as "a track worn by a wheel or by habitual passage; a groove in which something runs." One good example of a rut or groove is evident in the old vinyl musical recordings, which have been replaced by CDs. When playing these records, the needle would come down into the groove of the record and, stuck there, it would play the tune from beginning to end as the turntable revolved. Did the needle stray out of the groove and play something else? No, it was stuck in the groove and always played the same tune over and over every time it was inserted in the groove. It was stuck in a habitual passage.

Mentally, we also often get stock in a habitual passage, playing the same old tune over and over. In reprogramming ourselves, we must get out of the same old rut, the same habitual passage. This is often difficult, but it can be done. It takes desire, determination, and a plan. Your PPP is your plan. Follow it, and you'll make new grooves. You'll get out of the same old rut Timothy Leary said, "If you don't like what you're doing, you can always pick up your needle and move to another groove."

Let's look at some more examples of ruts, grooves, or habitual passages to illustrate the point. You've probably heard of traffic patterns. Every home, office, or building has them. A traffic pattern is the route most frequently taken in getting from one place or area to another. If you have carpeting in your home or office, you can easily see that your

A traffic pattern is the route most frequently taken in getting from one place or area to another.

traffic patterns become established after time as

the carpet becomes soiled or wears out. There is nothing wrong with traffic patterns; they normally demonstrate the best method of getting from here to there. But, if you realize you always take the same route in other areas of your life just because you've always done so, you may be stuck in a rut.

Many traffic routes and roadways became just that, routes and roadways due to habitual passage of travelers, horses, cattle, wagon trains, and early vehicles. Over time, these ruts or grooves in the landscape eventually became our highways of today. It was easier to follow the old roadways and make them into our present highways than to abandon the old familiar grooves for brand-new routes. It is always easier to follow the beaten path than to strike out in a new direction. Observe your daily routines. If you notice that you follow a habitual passage for the simple reason that you've always done so, you may want to examine it to see if you're doing it by choice or merely because of habit.

When I visited the towns of Garmisch-Parkenkerken in Bavaria, I was amazed at the daily ritual of the cows. Every morning the farmers let their cows out of their stalls and, unaided by human guides, the cows ambled through the center of Parkenkerken, often stopping to drink at the town's fountains in the middle of the street, and then they continued on up the mountainside to graze. In the evening, the entire scene played in reverse. At exactly the same time each day, the cows started down the mountainside, stopped briefly at the fountains to drink, and then they ambled back to their individual home stalls. The cows were

With your PPP, change can be accomplished easily.

practicing their daily habitual passage. There was no way that those cows, programmed to conformity, would ever take a different route.

We, too, are programmed to conformity, and if we want to change, it is necessary that we make new grooves for the new behaviors, beliefs, habits, and attitudes that we want to manifest or become evident in our lives. Trying to do it haphazardly, without a plan, will not work. But, with your PPP, change can be accomplished easily. First, your affirmations, which represent your goals and aspirations for a better future are carefully planned and wanted by you personally. They are yours and yours alone and obviously undertaken with sincere desire and determination. Second, by utilizing your PPP through constant repetition, your purpose will be accomplished quickly and easily, almost without your realizing it.

Repetition

Your PPP is your method of reprogramming. It will create new grooves, which, in time, will be-

Repetition is the golden key to success. come your new habitual passages. Remember, you wrote the script to depict your chosen future down to the last detail, so you can feel secure in, and look forward to, the expected results with total confidence.

Repetition is the golden key to success in this venture. The more you listen, and the more consistently you listen, the better. This is the major principle behind successful advertising. If it works for Madison Avenue and all the products and services you hear about on radio, see on TV, and read about in print, it will work for you.

I really feel that I can speak with authority in this area. I was actively involved with radio and television advertising and sales for twenty years. I sold airtime, wrote commercials, did live and taped television commercials and radio voice-overs, and portrayed countless characters in radio production spots. In addition to being fun and exciting, it was great training and, ultimately, very rewarding to me. I found that once the message was right, the factor that contributed the most to success in radio and television advertising was repetition of the commercial. Repetition is the key to successful advertising, just as it will be your key to success with your Personal Power Plan.

There are many variations on the repetition theme, too many to mention here. The important thing, with advertising or any message you hear or listen to, and unlike newspaper or print, which you see, is consistent repetition. Let's face it, the advertiser is trying to program your mind so that you'll act on his message. That is why, in order to succeed with your PPP, the personalized message you hear or listen to and choose to act on, must be consistently repeated until the message becomes firmly established in your subconscious.

You may say, "I never listen to commercials." Or, "I never pay attention to commercials, I tune out." You may not be actively listening, you may think you tune out, but your subconscious is recording the whole thing. Why do you think you pick one product over another in the supermarket? Something in your subconscious helps you choose because, perhaps unknowingly, you've heard of it. Why do you pass over brand after brand? Probably because you never heard of them. Why, when looking for a special type of business or service in the yellow pages, do you choose one over the otter? Perhaps you heard one of their commercials without even realizing it. Hearing something repeatedly is the key to successful advertising.

Repetition is the key to action. Repetition makes claims believable. If you hear anything repeated often enough, eventually you begin to believe what you've heard. That's another reason why your PPP is so very powerful. After suffi-

A key word or brief phrase, repeated several times mentally or verbally, can have the same effect as your longer version.

cient repetitions, you will believe your message and you will act on it. You will become the person you want to be, you will achieve your goals, and you will manifest your desires.

Perhaps you do watch TV commercials or listen to them on the radio only to berate them. Some may irritate you tremendously. But look at what happens when you go to the store. You buy something you've heard of because you feel more confident with the known, the familiar. You may hate die commercial, but you still act on it.

Advertising is what keeps radio and television stations and their programs on the air. National advertisers have enormous budgets for their products. They know a successful campaign can make or break a product. Campaigns would not be undertaken nor millions spent if repetitive advertising did not work. The fact is that it does work and that's been proved beyond any doubt. Let the repetitive factor work for you in your life.

If you pay attention to commercials, you will note that many with the same message or theme have more than one length or version. You may have been programmed for a time with a sixty-second spot. Then, because the message is firmly established in your mind, the advertiser can run a shorter version, perhaps ten or twenty seconds in length. This saves the advertiser the more expensive sixty-second rate yet, because of the workings of your subconscious mind, you mentally replay the longer version when you hear the short one. Just a brief mention can bring back the entire message. The effect is the same as if you'd heard the full-length spot.

This is an important concept to remember when dealing with affirmations. Perhaps for some reason you're unable to listen to your PPP tape, yet you want to take advantage of the repetitive factor. A key word or brief phrase, repeated several times mentally or verbally, can have the same effect as your longer version. So, after listening to your tape for a sufficient length of time to imprint your subconscious, you can cash in on the time spent, so to speak, by utilizing abbreviated affirmations anywhere and anytime. Just as with the examples of the radio and TV commercials, you'll reap the full benefit of your previous listening.

A key word or brief phrase, repeated several times mentally or verbally, can have the same effect as your longer version.

Actually, you've been making use of the repetitive factor all of your life. How did you learn the alphabet or your multiplication tables? By repetition, of course. That's how you memorize and learn just about everything—songs, speeches, playing the piano—you name it. Repetition is what gets the job done. If you really want to get something in your head for keeps, you practice it over and over. Listening to your PPP repetitively will permanently imprint your goals and desires in your subconscious mind and that obedient servant will go to work on your behalf to see that your personal message will soon become a reality.

A final thought on the power of repetition: Recently I attended a speaker's meeting in which one of the speakers on the program discussed the making of an inspirational speech. We listened carefully to Martin Luther King, Jr's famous seven-minute "I Have a Dream" speech. Members of the audience were asked to comment on why that particular speech was so dynamic and memorable.

Many factors were pointed out, of course, but the one that stuck in my mind is that in this relatively short speech, King repeated his key phrase, "I have a dream," nine times. Suppose he had said "I have a dream" once or perhaps only two or three times. Do you think the speech would have had the same impact? Would we remember that phrase to this day if he'd said it only once or twice? Of course not. The impact was delivered by the mental pictures he projected into the minds of the listeners and by the repetition of his key phrase, "I have a dream." That phrase is imprinted in the minds of the people of the United States because of

Listen, and watch your dreams come true.

the man, the situation, and the repetition. Those four words always have an instant reaction and they will always be identified with Martin Luther King, Jr.

What are your dreams? I hope you've included all of them in your PPP. Make them a reality by listening to your PPP tape repetitively, day in and day out. Listen, and watch your dreams come true.

14

Customize It

Scripts for Special Purposes

*E*ven though you might think every area and facet of your life has now been covered in a balanced manner by the Six Arenas of Life, on occasion something unusual or out of the ordinary is bound to come up and require attention. That's when you may want to consider preparing a customized special purposes tape.

Over the period of time that I've been working on this book, people who've heard that I do tapes have called upon me to prepare special tapes for them to meet their unique needs. And, in some cases, I've offered to write and record a script when I thought it would be helpful for someone in a particular dilemma or because of unusual circumstances. I'll give you a few examples.

My cousin was suffering from a chronic condition that baffled the doctors. Her worry and concern only aggravated matters and the condition continued to worsen. Because she is a very private person, I felt she would prefer not to discuss the problem with me except in very general terms. It was my opinion that her condition was mind/body related and that reprogramming her subconscious mind

It was my opinion that reprogramming her subconscious mind in certain areas would be beneficial.

in certain areas would be beneficial. I knew she was under a tremendous amount of stress due to the deadline for a serious project that was of great importance to her. Since I knew her family and background well, I undertook the challenge of preparing a healing tape for her, without her specific input; I hoped it would be helpful in boosting her self-esteem and positive outlook, clarifying her goals, and giving her a measure of peace of mind during a difficult period and thus alleviate the problem.

I do not suggest doing this as a general rule; that is, acting without the request or the personal input of the individual concerned. But, as I always say to those for whom I prepare tapes, "This tape has been prepared for you with love. I hope you will utilize it but, if you don't want to,

It is the overall meaning that counts. that's quite all right. If any of the words or phrases are not to your liking, simply ignore them.

It is the overall meaning that counts. The script I taped for my cousin, which was in four sections, is as follows:

General Affirmations

I am the best that I can be. I do whatever is necessary to improve myself.

I always maintain a positive mental attitude.

Every day in every way I am getting better and better.

I am optimistic and confident in all that I do.

I am the master of my fate, I am the captain of my soul.

I affirm only the best for myself and others.

I am the creator of my life and my world.

I am confident, self-assured, and optimistic.

I am worthy to receive all that I ask.

I deserve to be happy, healthy, prosperous, and successful.

I am relaxed, serene, comfortable, and confident.

What I believe about myself is what I will become. I believe the best.

I am transformed by the renewing of my mind.

Goals

I am in possession of my goals. My subconscious mind will guide me toward their manifestation.

I am in full control of my life.

I make right decisions quickly and easily.

I meet daily challenges gracefully and with complete confidence.

I accept total responsibility for my life, thoughts, and actions.

I have all the energy I need to accomplish my goals and to fulfill my desires.

Spiritual

I choose to experience peace of mind.

I allow higher wisdom to direct and guide me.

The universe nurtures and supports me at all times and in all places.

All things are working for good in my life.

I am relaxed knowing my higher self is providing me with whatever wisdom, guidance, and healing I need at this time.

I release my fears and insecurities and replace them with faith and confidence.

I am truly blessed in every area of my life.

Health Oriented

I fill my mind with positive, nurturing, and healing thoughts.

My peaceful and tranquil thoughts relax and soothe every inch of my body.

I am restored and revitalized.

God's love heals me and makes me whole.

My body is healed, restored, and filled with energy.

My body is perfect in every way.

I am healthy and strong. Every cell in my body functions perfectly.

My thoughts are positive, healing, and nurturing.

My sleep is relaxed and refreshing.

I sleep well and always awake feeling refreshed and rejuvenated.

I am in radiant good health. I feel great!

My body is healed, restored, and filled with energy.

A miracle of total healing is occurring now.

I taped the above segments in the three personal pronouns as explained previously, that is, using you or your, and then using my cousin's first name. Theresa, whom I mentioned earlier, wanted two things in her life: a husband and a state of prosperity. She asked me to make a tape for her that would attract both the right man and prosperity into her life. She was very specific in the input she gave me for the husband. For the prosperity message and because she is a very spiritual person, I utilized wording appropriate for that aspect of her being. Her scripts follow. On side 1 of the tape I prefaced her messages with the following:

Listen to this tape at least twice daily, in the morning upon arising, in the evening before retiring, and additionally as often as possible throughout the day. Live with the certainty that your desires, or demands, as they are often referred to in metaphysical terminology, will manifest for you. Act as if you have already received and give thanks that what you requested is *Make the demand for your divine selection and for what is yours by divine right.* yours now. It is important to have an attitude of gratitude. Do not discuss your project with others whose doubts may dilute its effectiveness. Communicate only with the infinite spirit or the god within. Always phrase your requests or demands correctly. Remember, every desire, whether spoken or unexpressed, is a demand. Make the demand for your divine selection and for what is yours by divine right.

That is important because you do not want something or someone that is not rightfully yours. You do not want to receive at the expense of others. There is plenty for all. And, you most certainly do not want to receive at the expense of yourself by, for example, receiving money m the way of an insurance payment for an accident or injury, or death of a loved one. Problems are eliminated by stating, "under grace in a perfect way," which removes any doubt about the quality of your request. It makes clear that you request only what is for the greatest good of all concerned and with harm to no one.

> *It is important to have an attitude of gratitude.*

For the Husband

> The man I am now attracting into my experience is single, successful, and financially secure.
>
> He is able to take care of me materially and emotionally.
>
> He is kind and generous to me and my family.
>
> He is strong, spiritual, and loving.
>
> His hair, eyes, and complexion are appealing to me. I admire his entire appearance. Physically, he is everything I desire in a man.

He is able to express his feelings freely. Any feelings of anger are expressed in a constructive manner.

He lets me be my own person and he loves me for being that person.

He wants to be married to me and live with me in this city.

The man I am how attracting into my experience is my soul mate, a mirror of myself.

1 will know him when I see him. He is the divine selection for my life.

Infinite Spirit, open the way for the divine selection, the right man, to come to me under grace in a perfect way. I taped Theresa's "Husband" message on one side of her tape. And, as with my cousin's tape, I utilized the three-persons method—you and her first name, Theresa. I put the "Prosperity" message on the other side of her tape. I prefaced it with the following:

The following are affirmations designed to increase your prosperity consciousness and thereby bring prosperity into your life. Each one will be repeated three times. Feel free to speak along with the tape. Some affirmations will have a greater significance for you than others. For greater impact, you may want to write those on cards and place them where you will see them frequently through-out the day.

Prosperity

God is my unfailing supply and large sums of
money come to me quickly under grace in
perfect ways. (Shinn)

Infinite Spirit, open the way for my ever-increasing prosperity. I am an irresistible
magnet for all that belongs to me by divine
right.

Unlimited prosperity now flows to me in a
steady, ever-increasing stream of success,
happiness, and abundance.

The Universal Spirit of Prosperity is providing
richly for me now. I am filled with gratitude.

God is the source of my unlimited supply, and
He is constantly opening new channels of
prosperity to me. I am open, receptive, and
thankful.

Unlimited supply is flowing to me now from
all points of the universe.

Everything that belongs to me by divine right
is now released and comes to me in great
avalanches of abundance under grace in
miraculous ways.

Infinite Spirit, I now give thanks for increased
prosperity in every area of my life.

It has been said, "Ask and it shall be given
   you, seek and you shall find, knock and it
   shall be opened unto you."

With faith, I shall ask, seek, and knock.

Paul said, "Faith is the substance of a thing hoped
   for, the evidence of a thing unseen." I know
   my faith will bring the things I hope for—
   which are yet unseen—into manifestation.

Christ said, "All things whatsoever you pray
   and ask for, believe that you receive them
   and you shall have them."

I believe.

I am thankful for the gifts received with all my
   heart and soul. I accept with gratitude, happiness, and strengthened faith. I am "transformed by the renewing of my mind."

Recently, a close friend told me that her sister
was diagnosed with a terminal illness and was
given a year to live. I offered to make a tape for
her sister in the hope that, through the mind/
body connection and the power of her subconscious mind, a reversal could be effected. At the
very least, it was hoped that her life expectancy
would be extended. I recorded the following:

Daily I fill my mind with positive, nurturing,
   and healing thoughts.

My peaceful and tranquil thoughts relax and
   soothe every inch of my body.

I am restored and vitalized.

God's love heals me and makes me whole.

My body is healed, restored, and filled with energy.

My body is perfect in every way.

I am healthy and strong. Every cell in my body functions perfectly.

My thoughts are positive, healing, and nurturing.

I sleep well and always awake feeling relaxed, refreshed, and rejuvenated.

I have a right to be healthy. In my body there is an ever-present force for renewal in each and every cell.

I have the will to be well. Every day in every way I am growing stronger and stronger.

Because I have faith, I see wholeness where there appears to be sickness. My faith is not simply the desire to be whole. It is not just the hope that somehow God will heal me. My faith is the perception of wholeness, the intuitive sense of being whole even in the midst of sickness. If I truly believe in my healing, I shall receive my healing. I now act as if this has come to pass. I believe.

I am innately divine, whole, and complete. Therefore, the potential for a complete and total healing lies within me.

It has been said, "Ask and you shall receive; seek and you shall find." These are sacred promises. I now ask for renewed health. I seek, within the marvelous workings of my body, the perfect cure. I have absolute faith that these things, the perfect cure and renewed health, will come to pass.

What I believe about myself and my condition will manifest.

I believe I have the power to overcome my illness I believe that, once again, I can truthfully say, "I am in radiant good health!"

At this time, I choose to experience peace of mind.

I allow higher wisdom to direct and guide me.

I am relaxed, knowing my higher self is providing me with whatever wisdom, guidance, and healing I need at this time.

I now release, all of my fears and replace them with faith and confidence.

I am transformed by the renewing of my mind and by my faith.

I expect a miracle of total healing to occur at any moment.

I am confident and at peace.

As with the others, I taped this three times using the first person as written, you, and then the young woman's first name. This script can be adapted for any illness or injury. I revised it recently to suit the special needs of another friend.

At a particular time in my personal life I felt the need for a special purpose tape to help me through a difficult situation. I have a thing about separation. I don't like it. I don't suppose anyone likes to be separated from someone they love, but I don't handle it well. I expect it goes back to my days as an Air Force wife when my pilot husband was always flying off into the wild blue yonder to fight wars and for special assignments.

I would be left home alone, wherever home happened to be at the time, with first one, then two, little ones and our dog. Back in those days—and I'm referring to World War II and the years immediately after—the Air Force located many of its bases in what I facetiously called ''garden spots.'' Actually, I enjoyed most of our assignments; it's just that home was not always what and where, in my wildest imagination, I had ever expected it to be.

One of our most interesting and challenging garden spots was Nome, Alaska. My husband, Campbell, was assigned there in 1948; his orders said "no dependents will accompany." I determined, "No one can stop us from going to Alaska!" And so three-year-old Beverly and I flew to Nome. Mickey, the Springer Spaniel, went along in the baggage hold.

In January of 1949, Campbell was sent stateside to learn more about fuels and lubricants. Although his primary duty was to fly, all pilots also had ground assignments and his was that of being fuels and lubricants officer. Beverly, Mickey, and I remained in Nome in our off-base home. We had to live off-base because we were not included in his orders.

Home, in this case, was a shack or cabin left over from the Alaskan Gold Rush.

Home, in this case, was a shack or cabin left over from the Alaskan Gold Rush. The owner, our landlord, realizing there would be some crazy wives who'd ignore the "no dependents" order as we did, moved a couple of these old shacks into Nome, fixed them up a bit, and offered them out as rentals. Our little Nome shack had no plumbing or running water, and therefore no bathroom, because pipes would freeze in the subzero temperatures. We bought water by the bucket from an Eskimo who came door to door when we placed our W for water sign in the window.

We stored this water in a receptacle built into the back wall of the kitchen. Because this wall faced north the water froze instantly when the norm wind blew. We then used an ice pick to chip off enough ice to melt in order to brush our teeth. Heat was provided by the kerosene cooking stove in the kitchen. We were allowed to buy kerosene from the base with special permission from the fuels and lubricants officer, my husband.

To make a long story short, Campbell flew away to the States and we stayed behind. January is usually the worst month of the year in Nome and, you guessed it, we got snowed in for several days. Fortunately, we had enough supplies to tide us over except for fuel; the small drum outside of the building only held so much. There was no way to stock up.

When it was gone, it was gone! It went dry about 3 a.m. Running out of fuel is a serious problem, not simply a matter of comfort, in an uninsulated dwelling when the temperature is fifty or more below zero and the wind is howling. It

becomes a matter of life and death. It got so cold inside that the china and glasses started cracking. In a panic, I called the base requesting an emergency, middle-of-the-night fuel delivery. Yes, we did have a phone, thank goodness. But guess what? I was told I needed the permission of the fuels and lubricants officer and he was stateside on temporary duty. How well I knew!

> *It got so cold inside that the china and glasses started cracking.*

Have you ever tried to deal with any branch of the government? And the Air Force is that, of course. I was told I was out of luck; Lieutenant Potter was the only one who could sign for the delivery. "Couldn't I, Mrs. Potter, sign his name?" I asked; I'd done it before. Obviously they could not allow an Air Force family to freeze to death so, after much pleading, a truck was sent out to fill our tank. A certain tragedy was averted.

That was a relatively minor separation; it only lasted about a month. There were many others of much longer duration and under more serious circumstances, namely a war or two. How well I remember the agony of saying good-bye at a train station and, later, an airport, never knowing how long Campbell would be gone or if he'd ever come home.

Originally the saying for draftees and those who enlisted was, "Good-bye dear, I'll be back in a year." Then it became "for the duration." The pain of separation is still so firmly embedded in

How well we are programmed!

me that I cannot watch a World War II movie without going to pieces. In fact, I now refuse to watch any vintage pictures that bring back those kinds of memories; it is simply too painful. Sometimes an old song can do it, too. How well we are programmed!

So, faced with a prolonged separation from someone I love dearly, all the old emotions started flooding back. Even before Hans left, the panic attacks began. The worst time was the middle of the night. I'd awake with a start and sit straight up in bed in terror. I'd hyperventilate, feeling that gut-wrenching emptiness, exactly the same as I'd experienced so many times so many years ago when the train pulled away from the station and I was left, still waving.

Can you believe this? Me in this dilemma? At first it never occurred to me to make a personal tape or write some affirmations for myself to deal with my personal issue. Was I suffering from a "Do as I say, not as I do" or "Too soon old, too late smart" syndrome? No. I simply had not thought of preparing a tape for this personal problem of mine. When I did, it was like the light bulb going on in my head. Of course! I can come to my own rescue. Here is the brief separation message that I prepared for myself:

I can cope; I always have, I always will.

I am in control of my thoughts and my emotions.

I am calm and rational rather than emotional.

I am strong; nothing can faze me.

I enjoy having time alone to think and plan.

I am the creator of my life and my world.

It is peaceful to be by myself.

I now do what I want to do when I want to do it.

I have time to start new projects and finish old ones.

I can read and write without interruption.

I now have time to meditate.

My life and my environment are very well organized.

I am in full control of my life.

I make right decisions quickly and easily.

I meet daily challenges gracefully and with complete confidence.

I always maintain a positive mental attitude.

I am relaxed, serene, comfortable, and confident.

I am not alone. God is with me.

He gives me comfort and guides me in all that I do.

I am truly blessed and I am grateful for my
  many blessings.

I know that God is watching over my loved
  ones at all times.

My loved ones are wrapped in the white light
  of divine protection, safe and free from
  harm.

I am at peace.

I put this on tape, reading each affirmation three
times. Sometimes I changed the inflection as I
read to reinforce the meaning. Then I repeated
the process two more times so that each affirmation was read nine times, making the tape a total
of twenty minutes in length. I did this to fit into
my own personal schedule; dealing with my face
and hair takes twenty minutes each morning,
doing the dishes usually takes twenty minutes,
and walking Charlie is a forty-minute operation.
During our walks, I play the tape twice.

Some of the affirmations are more meaningful
for my middle-of-the-night screaming meemies.
Those I have memorized and I repeat them sooth-
ingly to myself as needed. It's a take-off of the old
prescription, "Take two as needed and sleep well
until morning!" This was like a cram course and
I am pleased to report a remarkable success with
this set of affirmations. Ever since I began listening to this special tape, my sleep has improved
considerably.

The foregoing are examples of scripts for special occasions not covered by the six categories of your life arenas. I hope they prove to be helpful in demonstrating how to prepare personal customized scripts and tapes for any occasion or circumstance that may occur in your life.

15

Walking in Rhythm—
Make Your Cadence Count

Have you ever watched a parade or been in one? They say everyone loves a parade and I know that I certainly do. When I was a young girl I participated in many and, at the time, being in a parade was the most exciting thing I could think of doing. My father was in the military service during World War I and, because of that, he was active in veterans' organizations, most notably the American Legion, throughout his lifetime.

His American Legion post in Irvington, New Jersey, marched on every patriotic holiday and on any and every occasion anyone could think of to bring out the band, the flags, and the entire Irvington American Legion post in uniform.

The post also formed a drill team composed of the young daughters who were members of the auxiliary. When I grew big enough to fit into a uniform, I was allowed to join the team. I really thought I was hot stuff in my maroon and tan uniform trimmed with gold braid and brass buttons plus matching military hat held on by a gold learner strap under my chin.

I must say, as a drill team, we were pretty good. In addition to taking part in all of the local parades in honor of national holidays, we were invited to appear at American Legion conventions all over the state of New Jersey because we had won many local prizes for our marching and drill proficiency.

The reason for our success was Dad's friend, Al Tuttle, our drill team instructor. He ran us through our paces every Wednesday night in a high school gymnasium near the legion hall. Just like all the Army drill sergeants in the movies, he was relentless. "Hup, two, three, four! Hup, two, three, four! ALICE! You're out of step—two, three, four!" Once was all it took. Never again would I get out of step under the sharp and critical eye of Drill Sergeant Tuttle. He taught us well and we usually managed to execute our complicated maneuvers without a flaw in front of the reviewing stand.

What Mr. Tuttle was doing with his calling "Hup, two, three, four" was establishing the cadence—the beat* time, or measure of the march. Without the cadence, the marchers would not be able to keep in step with each other. If you've ever had the occasion to be on a military base, you've probably seen a group of recruits marching along the roadway with someone calling out

the cadence; sometimes they all call it out in unison. "Sound off—one, two. Sound off—-three, four.

Sound off—one, two—three, four." Occasionally, they'll all sing a marching song with a strong beat. It helps to keep them coordinated, in step, and in time with the beat, or cadence. Usually, at least to the onlooker, it looks as if they're enjoying it. Definitely, marching to a cadence does make it easier and more tolerable, if not enjoyable.

Utilizing a cadence can be very beneficial to you when working with your affirmations. A cadence provides a rhythmic sequence or flow to match affirmations worded with a beat in mind. When walking, exercising, or participating in any activity where there is a rhythm, beat, time, or measure, you might as well double your investment of time by affirming while you're participating in the activity.

Most of the time, throughout this book, I've been talking to you about listening to your personalized tape, the culmination of your PPP. And I certainly advocate your doing so with such activities as walking and exercising whenever possible. And, as I've said previously, listening consistently for a period of twenty-one days will begin to establish the message in your mind. Continued listening will reinforce the message and help to keep it firmly in the forefront of your mind. But, after a sufficient period of time, you can cut back on the frequency of listening to your PPP and incorporate other methods that will also reinforce your program.

The affirmation exercises and ideas in this chapter can be used at any time and anywhere without the necessity of listening to your tape. Obviously there will be

The affirmation exercises can be used at any time and anywhere.

Walking is an easy and convenient exercise for most people. You simply step outside your front door and start. times when you won't have your tape with you or you don't have access to a cassette player. That's when you'll want to employ these ideas in order to doubly reinforce your personal reprogramming.

Walking is an easy and convenient exercise for most people. You simply step outside your front door and start. No special equipment; no going to the gym; no changing into tights, leotards, or swimsuits; and no waiting for vacant exercise machines. All you need are your regular clothes and comfortable shoes. You just start walking, as briskly as possible, and keep going for as long as you like. You can walk year round in most places and, when it gets too cold, too snowy, or too icy, head for the nearest mall and walk there.

While walking briskly, remember my drill sergeant, Al Tuttie, and get that "Hup, two, three, four" cadence in your mind. Then, think of an affirmation that you particularly want to enforce, and put it to the beat. For example, if reading more books is something you've promised yourself to do, you may want to get that message into a cadence or beat. "I read—two—books—each—month." The "I read" is said rapidly, followed by "two—books—each—month." The last four words are said individually as each foot hits the pavement: left—right—left—right."

An affirmation that I used for a long time with the cadence principle when I wanted to lose a few pounds went like this: "I weigh one-twenty, I weigh one-twenty." I just re-peated it over and over in time with the "Hup, two, three, four" cadence. "I weigh one-twenty— I weigh one-twenty." Grad-ually, guess what? I weigh one-twenty! You see, when I stood on the scale and the dial registered a figure oth-er than one-twenty, I knew something was wrong. My subconscious said I weigh one-twenty. Without realizing I was doing anything about it, I must have cut down slight-ly on my food intake, or I walked more, or I walked faster. Remember that old saying, "The devil made me do it?" In this case, my subconscious made me do it. Before too long, the scale registered one-twenty and it's been there ever since. The cause was my affirmation; the effect was attaining the weight I desired.

About the same time as the "one-twenty" experience, I was between relationships. I was seeking a new partner and, after learning about the universal principles discussed earlier in this book, I knew I could attract a new partner, one who would be appropriate for me, through the like attracts like principle. I thought long and hard about the characteristics I wanted in a new partner. I encapsulated those characteristics into the phrase "perfect partner." My walking affirmation became "I now attract a perfect partner." The "I" was said quickly, and the "now—attract—perfect—partner" were said in cadence: "now—attract—perfect—partner" or left—right—left—right, as my feet hit the pavement.

Was my perfect partner attracted into my life? You bet he was! The law of expectation was at work here. I believed I could attract a perfect partner into my life. Because I believed it, I expected it to happen. Therefore, I went about my life and activities with an air of expectancy about me. I exuded the vibe, as we used to say in the sixties. I approached every new man with friendly expectancy, excitement, anticipation, and openness. I participated in activities that I enjoyed. After all, my perfect partner would be involved in doing the same things that I liked to do and, most of all, I made myself visible. It's not very often that one's Prince or Princess Charming comes knocking at the front door, although I've heard of a few times that it actually happened.

Another walking affirmation that I like a lot because it covers a number of bases is, "I'm happy, healthy, wealthy, and wise." Again, the "I" is said rapidly and the "happy, healthy, wealthy, ('and' is said quickly, if at all) wise" are said to your beat or cadence. "Happy—healthy—wealthy—wise." Left—right—left—right. Am I happy, healthy, wealthy, and wise? Well, these attributes are up for individual interpretation, especially the wealthy part. Wealth is not necessarily measured in terms of finances. So, for me, according to my personal definition gained after much introspection, the answer is yes, most definitely.

Here's an affirmation that I know is imprinted on my sub-conscious mind forever. "I'm in radiant good health." I affirmed, "I'm in radiant good health" for several months during my daily walks and I felt really great. I still do. Some time later, during a routine checkup, my doctor noted a slightly higher than normal blood pressure reading. "That's absurd, Doctor," I told him in astonishment, "I'm in radiant good health," as if to say, "How dare you suggest otherwise?" The words "I'm in radiant good health" just popped out of my mouth to my complete surprise. You might say I programmed myself to be in radiant good

What you believe does come true for you.

health. I feel as if I'm in radiant good health and I'm told that I look as if I'm in radiant good health. I'm happy about both of those observations which incidentally, are true. Note the use of as if in the previous sentence. Remember our discussion of the law of expectation?

What you believe does come true for you. Please note that I am not suggesting that you delude yourself with overly positive affirmations, especially in the area of health. Of course you will listen to your medical advisor and attend to any problems that he or she might point out. If you do not, affirming good health in the face of obvious problems could create deceptive beliefs and delay appropriate treatment. I am a strong advocate of the mind/body connection and suggest that a positive, optimistic attitude when faced with illness or disease will help to facilitate healing and recovery. And what about my blood pressure? It was borderline, but it has been corrected by the reduction of salt in my diet.

If you have a long affirmation that is not conducive to a beat, condense it into a few words or a phrase that fits your walking rhythm and that, to you, encompasses me meaning of the entire affirmation. It will have the same result, that is it will sink into your subconscious because you know the full wording and intended meaning.

I am particularly drawn to biblical promises, which I like to use as affirmations. Because some phrases from *The Bible* do not fit a cadence or beat, I use the aforementioned suggestion and condense the passage mat inspires me. For example, "Ask and it shall be given you; seek and you shall find." I really believe these words and, if they are meaningful to you, too, you might abbreviate them like this: "Ask—receive. Seek—find." These four words now fit nicely into a cadence for use while walking or exercising.

The cadence principle can also be used along with most of the exercises you might do at a gym or health club, or when exercising at home. Every gym I ever belonged to used taped or recorded music as an adjunct to the group exercises. This is done for a number of reasons. It keeps the group together, that is, exercising in unison, and it increases the energy level of the participants and in the room. It also makes exercising more fun and less boring.

Affirming to music can also be more fun and less boring. Just as with your walking affirmations, when exercising, you phrase your affirmations to fit the beat of the music being played or to the instructor's count. It may take a bit more concentration on your part to tune out the lyrics or the instructor's count, but that only makes for stronger affirmations and better results. Leg lifts, crunches, push-ups, and sit-ups become doubly productive when an affirmation is added. You can affirm while using free weights, too, because, being a rhythmic activity, using free weights is conducive to counting to a cadence or the beat of the background music.

The gym offers a perfect setting for utilizing the affirmations that you scripted in your Physical category. A great overall affirmation to use in the gym, or anywhere else for that matter, is Emile Coue's famous phrase, "Every day in every way, I'm getting better and better." "Every day—every way—getting better—and better." Whether you're lifting your leg as in leg lifts, or a weight when using free weights, you follow

For the gym: "Every day in every way, I'm getting better and better."

an up—down—up—down sequence. The process is very similar to that used when walking with the left—right—left—right foot placement in time with a beat or cadence. Here's another physical affirmation that I like for overall gym work: "Stronger—slimmer-lighter—tighter." Up— down—up—down. "Stronger slimmer—lighter— tighter."

But don't think affirmations done at the gym need to be strictly about your physical well-being. That's only logical, but you should feel free to affirm anything you please at any time no matter where you are. When I was affirming for a perfect partner, believe me, that was my primary affirmation everywhere I went. Also, whenever I feel a cold coming on, my old faithful "I'm in radiant good health" becomes my primary affirmation at the gym, on my walks, even in the middle of the night if I happen to wake up. In addition to impacting my subconscious, I believe it has a direct effect on my immune system, therefore I am, and expect to remain, in radiant good health.

Turn on your favorite radio station, put an upbeat musical cassette or CD into your player, hum or sing out loud or to yourself, or mentally call out a military cadence and get with the beat. Word your affirmations to the beat and let them go to work for you. Never, never miss an opportunity. Walk in rhythm, exercise in rhythm, think in rhythm. The more you do, the faster you'll have the desired results.

16

Rhythm and Rhymes—

Jingle, Jangle, Jingle

Remember the old Bing Crosby song that goes, "I've got spurs that jingle, jangle, jingle as I ride oh so merrily along"? Let's change that to say, "I've got words that jingle, jangle, jingle as I stride oh so merrily along." Corny, maybe, but that's exactly what we're going to discuss in this chapter—the effect that a rhyme, jingle, or slogan—corny though it may be—can have in helping you remember important words and phrases. These work especially well for affirmations that you might use as you "stride oh so merrily along."

Rhymes, jingles, and slogans are far easier to remember than ordinary phrases. That's why they're used so frequently in advertising. Madison Avenue knows that if it can get us humming or singing along with their message, they've got us hooked. For a fun exercise, I started thinking about old jingles, slogans, and mottos and came up with the following. Some are many decades old and, if you don't recognize them, you're obviously much younger than I. Take a look and see if any of them start you reminiscing.

Rinso White—Sponsor of soap operas in the thirties.

Call for Philip Morris —Remember Johnny?

J-E-L-L-O—Jack Benny on Sunday nights.

Lucky Strike Green has gone to war—WW II.

Snap, Crackle, Pop—Kellogg

Pepsi Cola hits the spot—12 full ounces, that's a lot!—Pepsi

Cola is the drink for you—
Pepsi before Michael Jackson

This Bud's for you—Budweiser

Wouldn't you really rather drive a Buick?

Fly the friendly skies—United

We love to fly and it shows—Delta

Take the bus and
leave the driving to us—Greyhound

A little dab'll do ya—Brylcreem

Where's the beef?—Wendy's

When you care enough
to send the very best—Hallmark

Don't leave home without it
—American Express credit card

You'll love it at Levitz—furniture

What a difference a day makes—C& R Clothiers

I've fallen and I can't get up!
—Mrs. Fletcher and Life Alert

Just say "NO"—Nancy Reagan

What are your favorites? I'll bet you can come up with a bunch also. The point is, if I can remember these—and some are as much as fifty years old—it's obvious that jingles, rhymes, and slogans have an impact. I know they're imprinted in my mind.

Songs have the same effect. I can remember most of the words from many of my favorite songs of the forties and fifties, even the sixties. After that, I seem to have tuned out for the most part. The important thing to recognize here is that rhyming makes things easier to renumber, and those memories remain. I expect I'll still be able to sing along with my old favorites when I'm in my dotage.

Put this factor to work for you. If you have trouble remembering your affirmations when you're without your PPP tape, condense them into snappy slogans or into a rhyming message.

Pretend you're an advertising copywriter and it's your job to come up with easy-to-remember phrases for your most important personal statements. When I was an advertising copywriter, I tended to overdo this because it was so much fun. I was often teased about putting everything in rhyme. My answer to that was:

> It's not a crime
> to make things rhyme!

This is not a new theory that advertising copywriters, big and small, dreamed up. Others have used the same principle. Thomas Edison, the famous inventor, was, to use a nineties term, an energy conserving person, and he was probably a bit frugal besides. He didn't want his precious light bulbs burning away for no purpose. Hung from the electric light chain in his recording room was a sign that read:

> Save the juice, save the juice.
> Turn out the lights when not in use.

In her beautiful and inspiring little book, *The Game of Life and How to Play It*, Florence Scovel Shinn frequently recommends rhyming as an easy and effective way to word affirmations. In counseling a woman who came to her for advice in finding an appropriate job that paid a decent wage, Shinn suggested this affirmation:

> I have a perfect work
> In a perfect way;
> I give a perfect service
> For a perfect pay.

The wording clicked with the woman, and she sang the words to herself throughout the day. Before long, she found her perfect work, for which she gave a perfect service and received a perfect pay. She found it in a perfect way because she affirmed and believed she would. Her contribution was a perfect service, which was critical to her receiving a perfect pay.

Shinn stresses the necessity of wording your affirmations in ways that click for you, and I agree wholeheartedly. If your wording is stilted, hard to remember, or doesn't flow readily—if it doesn't click—you'll stumble over the affirmation and therefore render it useless. Work over the words until they come easily and flow smoothly. That's why putting your affirmations into the form of rhymes can be fun as well as effective. After playing around for a few minutes, I came up with some rhymes to help get you started.

For the work I do
I get praise. So—
On a regular basis,
I get a good raise.

Two—four—six—eight
Who do I appreciate?
Me! Cause I'm losing weight
And I'm feeling really great!

Hip, hip, hooray!
This is my day—
I'm a winner in every way!

The books I read
Help me succeed.

Checks come in the mail;
Checks come in the mail.
Without fail—
Week in, week out,
Checks come in the mail.

"Checks come in the mail" is a statement used frequently by my daughter, Beverly. Although she's a psychologist with a Ph.D., she never had a desire to hang out a shingle for private clients or to practice psychology in a clinical setting. Being an entrepreneur and a bit of a maverick, she determined that she would do her own thing in her own way. In order to do so, she needed checks in the mail, so she put out the statement, "Checks come in the mail." Obviously she had to do something to create the checks that would come in the mail, and she did. Possibly it was her sub-conscious, her obedient servant that obeyed her "Checks come in the mail" message, and worked on her behalf to show her ways to accomplish that objective.

How did she do it? Some years ago, with the incredibly small sum of only $4,200, she was able to put a down payment on a piece of property with two small cottages on it in Palo Alto, California. For a time, she lived in one cottage and rented the other. Then the real estate market boomed and rents skyrocketed, so she moved out of her cottage and rented both, because her property was adjacent to a major university, the location commanded substantial rentals. Soon, she was able to purchase two more pieces of rental property and, with creative financing, she continues to add rental units and other properties to her portfolio. And the checks—rental checks—continue to come in the mail. This allows her to do what she wants to do at her own speed: to speak, to write and publish books, and to explore other entrepreneurial ventures that also cause checks to come in the mail.

When Beverly first mentioned her determination to have checks come in the mail and her success in receiving them, I thought, "What a great idea!" While I have a mild interest in real estate, I do not have the slightest desire to be a landlord bothered with tenants' complaints, plumbing problems, and property management, nor do I see myself dealing with the necessary paperwork and details that real estate investments require. I thought there must he an easier way for me to create checks in the mail.

My opportunity came with an unexpected financial windfall. It wasn't large but, instead of buying a new, expensive car as friends and family had been pestering me to do for years I invested it in a couple of dividend-producing products that now bring me checks in the mail. I probably would have splurged on the car. After all, I did need a better one, I rationalized, but a voice in my head wouldn't let me. It kept saying, "Checks come in the mail, checks come in the mail".

It also said, "I do whatever is necessary to achieve my financial goals." Yes, week in and week out, as my little rhyme promised, checks keep coming and my old car keeps going.

Actually, I'm rather fond of it—the car, that is. In order to have dividend checks come in the mail, I had to do something just as Beverly had to do something to have rental checks come in her mail. That's why my affirmation accompanied by "I do whatever is necessary" is so powerful.

It's the law of cause and effect in action. Beverly's investment in rental property was the cause, the rental checks were the effect. My investment in a financial product was the cause; the dividend checks were the effect. If you want to have checks come in your mail, do whatever is necessary to insure that outcome. Perhaps, like me, you don't have an inclination for real estate. Maybe you don't have the money to invest in a financial product. Put out the "checks come in the mail" affirmation as cause, if that's what you want, and allow your subconscious mind to direct you to the appropriate venture for you and you alone that will result in the effect, "checks come in the mail."

If rhyming or creating jingles doesn't come easily to you, regress in time to your childhood and remember the nursery rhymes that you grew up with. As far as I know, it's okay to plagiarize nursery rhymes because they're in public domain, that is they're no longer under copyright. If you had aspirations to be a magician, for example, you might paraphrase

> Jack, be nimble, Jack, be quick,
> Jack, jump over the candlestick.

to read:

> I am nimble, I am quick,
> I can fool them with every trick.

Everyone certainly remembers Jack and Jill, the couple that went up a hill.

> Jack and Jill went up a hill,
> to fetch a pail of water.
> Jack fell down and broke his crown,
> and Jill came tumbling after.

Here's a rhyming affirmative revision of "Jack and Jill"

> I can—I will—perfect my skill,
> and do what I think is proper.
> Time after time my decisions are sound.
> And life is increasingly better.

Can you stand one more?

> Jack Sprat could eat no fat,
> His wife could eat no lean.
> But, together, they licked the platter clean.

In the spirit of cooperation, as demonstrated by Mr. and Mrs. Sprat, I offer the following.

> Let it be known, working alone
> Will not produce your dream.
> But working together,
> You can do it as a team.

Now it's your turn. Don't worry if you feel silly. You're supposed to have fun with this. In fact, a little levity is to be encouraged. The last thing I want is for you to make a heavy project out of preparing your PPP and your affirmations. Just allow the words and phrases that are meaningful to you to bounce around in your head and the next thing you know.

You'll be feeling fine
cause you've made things rhyme!

Remember, Jesus said, "You must be as little children to enter the kingdom of heaven."

17

Getting Personal—

Your Personal Power Plan

Why go through this personal audio recording routine when there are prepared recordings already available on almost every conceivable subject from weight loss to increased sales, as well as many categories that are not all that conceivable, including many available in both spoken and subliminal form?

The answer is that these recordings are general, not personal. They cannot apply to you specifically any more than your newspaper or magazine horoscope or astrology forecast can apply to you and you alone. Sure, I read my horoscope when I come across it, but I can hardly believe that my

Capricorn horoscope also applies to all the other Capricorns on this planet—approximately one-twelfth of the world's population—on a single day or for a given time period. You've got to be kidding! In a very general way, perhaps, these horoscopes may apply, but in a personal way, never!

I'm not putting down astrology, astrologers, or the study of the effect of the moon, stars, and sun on human affairs. Since the beginning of time, countless numbers of people have put a great deal of faith in this science, including kings and other heads of state. I'm saying the general astro-logical forecast or horoscope that you find in your newspaper or magazine is just that, general. On the other hand, a detailed horoscope that takes all of your personal and individual data into consid-eration, such as the exact time and place of birth and all the other necessary information, is per-sonalized. No one else's horoscope is exactly like yours.

This analogy applies to recordings prepared for general use versus your Personal Power Plan, which is carefully thought out, script-ed, affirmed, and recorded for you and you alone. Your PPP does not apply to, nor is it

Your Personal Power Plan is carefully thought out, scripted, affirmed, and taped for you and you alone.

appropriate for, anyone else on the face of the earth any more than your personal horoscope, prepared by an experienced astrologer, applies to anyone else born under your sign.

In addition, prepared recordings—because they're general—make general assumptions. They have to. I am referring to self-help tapes here rather than those focused toward business and career. For example, in the category of weight loss, the scripts of many prepared tapes seem to assume that people who overeat, or wish to lose weight and find it difficult, suffer from a lack of self-esteem or use food to bolster themselves emotionally. This may apply in some cases but definitely not all.

Personally, if I indulge occasionally, it's because I love food and love to eat and I live with someone whose hobby is preparing gourmet food. Of course it's hard not to indulge when faced with a refrigerator full of goodies, but self-esteem and emotions have nothing to do with it. A weight-loss tape I purchased some years ago in order to lose a few pounds focused on the low self-esteem aspect to such a degree that I found myself

A subliminal recording, in which the message is usually concealed under the sounds of birds, waterfalls, waves, and other sounds of nature can be insidious.

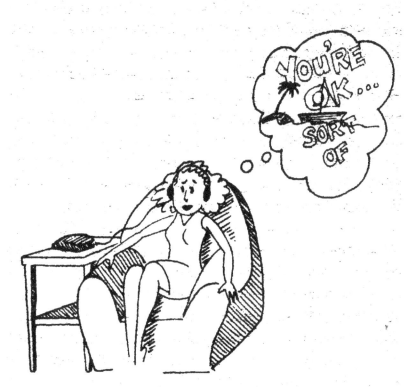

arguing furiously with the recording every time I listened. Any positive input was obviously canceled. However, when I implemented my Personal Power Plan, the unwanted pounds simply disappeared.

A subliminal recording, in which the message is usually concealed under the sounds of birds, waterfalls, waves, and other sounds of nature can be insidious in that you have little or no idea of the input. The content or theme of the tape is normally condensed in the recording title or a single sentence on the package.

You have no idea of the actual wording of the script that you're programming into your mental computer. Talk about scary! Your subconscious could be adversely affected if, as in the previous example, you're bombarded with poor self-esteem assumptions or any other assumed negative. In any case, your conscious mind will also pick up some of the input and, if it's contrary to your personal beliefs about yourself, you can be left confused and upset and your purpose in listening to the tape will not be accomplished.

This is not to say I'm against prepared programs. Nothing could be further from the truth. I'm a strong and definite proponent of tapes and the positive as well as educational benefits they can have on your thinking, attitude, perception, emotional well-being, and success in virtually every area of life. Because I'm such a pro-audio recording person, I have a substantial tape library covering a vast number of subjects that interest me. Many in the field of business were informative and helpful when I was in sales and managerial positions. Others in my personal tape library are on subjects that now interest me as a public speaker. Still others appeal in a very personal way as they address the inner me and my spiritual side. I often buy a favorite author's book on tape for easy listening while driving, doing mundane tasks, or walking my dog. Obviously, I'm a cassette person and think everyone can benefit from owning and listening to a well-rounded selection of recordings and albums.

Regardless of your aspirations in life, someone has undoubtedly produced a rrecording on the subject Many are excellent. If you are in the field of sales, for example, you can choose from dozens of well produced, informative, and effective cassette albums and individual tapes covering every aspect of the subject from prospecting and cold-calling to the art of persuasion and closing the sale. Take advantage of all that seem productive to you. Become an expert on sales. Learn all the necessary skills and techniques from experts in the field. Then, implement your personal sales goals and projections through your Personal Power Plan and, before long, you'll find yourself actually meeting the goals and projections you have chosen for yourself.

Good affirmations that combine the effects of both prepared sales programs and your PPP are, "I keep well informed on all aspects of the field of successful sales. I utilize all means at my disposal to do so. I always meet my sales goals and quotas." Then, as explained earlier, it's important to affirm specifics in the areas of goals and quotas so your subconscious mind can go to work for you to produce the exact result you wish to achieve.

There are many fine audio and video recording companies in the marketplace offering top quality programs and albums by bestselling authors, top speakers, and experts in many fields, so building a personal audio library can be a fun, rewarding thing to do. I heartily urge you to get started in this area if you haven't done so already. Catalogs and the internet are readily available for shopping by phone or mail; some companies even offer a thirty-day approval period. Most large bookstores have an audio section and specialty bookshops sometimes offer hard-to-find tapes on subjects such as metaphysics and holistic health.

I must warn you that, when purchasing audio what you buy is usually what you get. While some major companies such as Nightingale-Conant allow a thirty-day free trial period on albums, this does not apply to single or double recordings you buy from your local book or record store, even the large chains. They will usually only accept a CD for return or exchange if it is defective in some way. You're simply stuck if the program turns out to be not to your liking. There are some exceptions, of course. Some record shops allow you to preview a recording, usually musical, before buying. And, I've frequented some small metaphysical shops that have testers that you can listen to before making a decision. This is because their stock is so limited that they can handle it. Obviously, this would not be feasible at major bookstores.

As I mentioned earlier, these are all general programs, not personalized, and your benefits will therefore be general and not personal. Be well-rounded and pursue both avenues. But, for your very personal, very specific needs, the only recording that will do that job for you is your PPP, your Personal Power Plan.

18

It's All a Matter of Choice
The Choice Is Yours

I just survived an explosion! Don't worry, I wasn't hurt. Well, mentally, a bit, but physically I'm OK. What happened? I just came home from a shopping trip. Have you been in a big city department store lately? There are several that I frequent in San Francisco. Some occupy a full city block and are ten or more stories high. And what do they contain? Endless amounts of merchandise. Counter after counter, aisle after aisle, department after department, floor after floor of merchandise. What does that all add Up to? An infinite number of choices. It's a choice explosion! Enter a department store, and instantly you're bombarded from all sides with choices.

Choices of jewelry, cosmetics, accessories, casual domes, business attire, formal apparel, lingerie, cookware, appliances, silver and fine china, furniture, carpeting, and bedding. Going shopping definitely contributes to choice overload. It can boggle the mind and leave you feeling as if you've survived some sort of battle. I call it choice fatigue.

But exposing oneself to such an experience, be it exhilarating or wearing, is also a choice. Ah ha! There's that word again, choice. Choosing not to undergo the department store experience opens up other choice vistas in the shopping arena.

You can utilize shop-by-mail catalogs, personal shoppers, errand runners, or simply abstain from buying. You may abstain from buying, but you can never abstain from making a choice. Choosing not to-choose is, in fact, making a choice. Choosing is a constant fact of life day in and day out. The more choices there are, the more chances there are to make wrong choices. For example, you can choose the wrong investments for your

Choosing not to-choose is, in fact, making a choice.

future, the wrong car for your lifestyle, the wrong school for your children, the wrong neighborhood for your family, and the wrong spouse in the first place. Pick up any newspaper anywhere and much of what you'll read is about the wrong choices being made by upset, angry, desperate people everywhere in the world. These poor choices result in death, destruction, depression, and despair—in other words, headlines. Wrong choices make headlines; right choices seldom do.

What is the point? The point is that we all are constantly being faced with making choices, large and small, important and inconsequential, good and bad. How do you do in the choice department? Or, do you feel that what happens to you is done to you by people and circumstances, and you have little or no say about your experiences, station in life, and the events of your existence?

We all are constantly being faced with making choices, large and small.

Do you feel you have no choice, no control? Do you feel stuck in a boring, unchallenging, low-paying job, with a wife or husband who no longer cares or doesn't understand you, in a community devoid of opportunity, facing a future that is bleak and without hope? Do you feel that people and circumstances outside of your control have control over you and your life?

Martin said to me, "What can I do about it? I have to work. Nobody else is going to pay my bills. What choice do I have? Actually, I hate my job—have for years—but I can't quit or change now. Where else would I go? Nobody else would take me On at my age. Besides, I've put in too many years on this job; I'm just hanging in there until retirement. The more I think about things, the more depressed I get."

Emily feels defeated in more ways than one. "Our marriage has been a drag for years. We barely talk to each other anymore. The only thing we do talk about—fight is more like it—is money. Maybe if we weren't pushed so hard financially. On top of it all," she continued, "We've got to worry about the kids, Things aren't the same as they were when we were young. We're really worried; scared is more like it. Guns, drugs, and sex. What's the matter with the schools these days? What happened to reading, writing, and arithmetic? I don't think they're learning any of that. In fact, they can hardly spell! And no one seems to read anymore. But they'll still have to go to college or they'll be even worse off then we are. God knows how we're going to pay for it, even wife fee two of us working. We have no choice. Looks like Sam's going to have to take on a second job,"

Sam responds, "Did Emily also tell you I drink too much—and I smoke? Yeah, I know it's not good for my health. But I'm under a lot of pressure. You know, life sure has handed us a dirty deal. It's the pits and there's not a damned thing we can do about it. That's the breaks, I guess. Or just plain bad luck. If you're not born with a silver spoon in your mouth, you just can't make it these days. Choice has nothing to do with it!"

Does any of this sound familiar to you? Does it seem feat life just happened to you while you were busy doing other things? Certainly you didn't choose this state of affairs, If you had anything to say about such matters as your job, your spouse, your community, your health, your future, and your children's future, your life would be very different. Your life would be the way you want it to be. You would be in charge.

Well, my friend, you are in charge. You were in charge all along and you are in charge now. You possess the greatest gift to mankind, as does everyone. You possess the power of choice. You may not want to believe what I have to say, but try to suspend judgment temporarily and just consider this: We are all where we are at this moment in time because of past choices. Our today is a summation of yesterday's choices. Our futures will be determined by today's choices. As Robert Fritz says in *The Path of Least Resistance*, "Firmly place the authority for the quality and direction of your life where it belongs: in your own hands."

That can be a bitter pill to swallow if you are unhappy with your situation in life. It is understandable to blame others and conditions over which you feel you have no control for your personal chaos, misery, and lack of success. But the fact is that each and every one of us must take individual responsibility for me quality and direction of our lives. We do have the power of choice. If we are unhappy or dissatisfied in any-way, we can choose to change or make changes in our lives and circumstances.

The importance of our choices-—moment to moment, day by day, and over a lifetime—is mind-boggling. Everything in our lives, from the most inconsequential to the most significant, is mere because of choices we have made in the past. In choosing, we make a choice between one of two alternatives.

At the doorway, we choose to go in or out; at the elevator, we choose to go up or down; at the traffic light, to stop or go. At the grocery store, we choose one size, brand, or color over the other; and at the check-out counter, we choose paper or plastic for the bagging. When dining out, we're offered the choice of smoking or nonsmoking sec-tions, ground pepper or none on our salads, reg-ular or de-cafe coffee; at the gas pump we choose regular or unleaded.

If you are at home, look around you. You choose the furnishings, the accessories, and whether or not the doors and windows are open or closed, the lights on or off in the room in which you are standing. Perhaps you say you did not choose the paintings on the wall or some of the artifacts on the shelf because you liked them especially. Perhaps not. Perhaps you choose them because they were the right color, the right price, or filled the appropriate space. Perhaps some of the items in your room were given to you and you choose to display them in order not to hurt the feelings of the giver.

Perhaps you are merely renting or otherwise occupying a room full of furnishings chosen by someone else. Nevertheless, if you are living mere, you made the choice to do so. Ultimately, it always comes down to the matter of choice—your choice.

Look into your closet and into your dresser drawers. How did all of those clothes get there? Somebody bought them and, in doing so, choices were made, if some items were gifts, you chose to keep them, to wear them, if you do, or at least to keep them in your closet and in your drawers. We could go on indefinitely with this exercise. Look into your purse and wallet, your desk, your kitchen cabinets, refrigerator, and medicine chest, Everything contained therein was chosen and placed there by choice, yours or someone else's.

Some of our choices are so insignificant that they carry little value in the scheme of things. Does it really matter that today you chose to wear a red tie over a blue one, closed pumps instead of sling-backs, a sweater rather than a jacket, or one lipstick instead of another? Probably not.

Choosing to cut or color one's hair or shaving off a beard or moustache may cause temporary unhappiness if you're dissatisfied with the result, but time will take care of these problems. It does take patience, but the displeasure resulting from such choices is merely temporary. 'This, too, shall pass" is a comforting phrase that applies to such minor calamities as well as to major happenings over which we seem to have little or no control.

Some choices have lasting results. One's chosen curriculum in school may have a lifetime effect. It is probably important that you choose to send out resumes regularly if you're looking for employment; that you choose to keep plugging along on that novel you're writing if you ever hope to get it published; to choose to make that extra sales call if you expect to meet your quota. If you fail, it is often because you did not choose to persevere.

The choice of a car may carry a good deal of weight in the area of choices because some vehicles are safer than others. The choice of friends and associates is always important; we are known by the company we keep. One's choice of residence, even though temporary, can be of importance, especially when one considers earthquakes, hurricanes, fires, tornados, and floods. And, frequently, neighbors play an important role in one's life. Any job, even a temporary one, can be significant in the long run; often a first job determines one's field of employment for years to come, if not for life.

Other choices can be of even greater importance: The choice of a career and goals; one's permanent or semipermanent residence; the choice of a spouse or close relationship; the choice to have, or not to have, children; The choice to drink or smoke or do drugs and, later perhaps, the choice to give up these unhealthy habits.

"OK," you say, "I realize I've made countless choices over the years, some good and some bad.

Now I'm stuck with them. Now I have no choice. I have no choice but to continue in my job, which I hate. I have to agree with the boss or I'll get fired: I'm fed up with my marriage but I'm stuck in it I have no choke. My wife will take me for everything I've got if I try to divorce her." Or, "My husband beats me, I'm an abused and battered wife, but he'll find me and kill me if I leave or go to the authorities. Don't tell me about choice. I have none.

Choice has nothing to do with my life at this point," you may say. On the contrary. You still have a choice. It may not be easy but you can choose to quit that job and look for another one. You can choose to speak up to the boss at the risk of getting fired. You can choose divorce and remove yourself from an unhappy marriage. You can choose to leave your abusive husband and save your life both physically and emotionally. Others have done so. If you do not, you have made the choice to remain in an intolerable situation that makes you miserable and can shorten your life.

If you do choose to remain in the undesirable situation, you still have a choice. You can choose to change your attitude or your perception toward the things and people m your life that are making it a living hell. It's not an easy job by any means but, if there are no alternatives, changing your outlook may be the only choice.

The Course in Miracles states, "The purpose of

this course is to help us recognize that we have a choice as to how we perceive ourselves, others and the world about us. We have a choice as to whether we experience peace or conflict. We have a choice as to whether we experience love or fear."

Many people are born with or into or found themselves placed in situations over which they had no choice. Some women are bitter because they were not born male. Some Blacks would prefer to be White. Short people often wish to be tall. Most heavy people wish to be slim. The handicapped or retarded certainly did not choose to be born with their conditions. The disabled person or accident victim, unless he or she were deliberately careless, did not choose to be injured, incapacitated, or deformed. While those in prison chose to break the law, which resulted in their incarceration, those in wartime internment and concentration camps did not make such a choice; they were imprisoned against their will. How can one, in all honesty, tell these individuals, especially those in such traumatic and catastrophic situations, that they have the power of choice?

Viktor Frankl addresses this succinctly in his classic bestseller, *Man's Search for Meaning,* a moving account of his life in the horrors of the Nazi death camps. As the preface states, Frankl, a long-time prisoner, found himself stripped to naked existence. His father, mother, brother and his wife died in camps or were sent to the gas ovens so that, excepting for his sister, his entire family perished. How could he—every possession lost, every value destroyed, suffering from hunger, cold and brutality, hourly expecting extermination—how could he find life worth preserving?"

Frankl answers, "Everything can be taken from a man but one thing: the last of the human freedoms—to choose one's attitude in any given set of circumstances, to choose one's own way."

We all have this freedom. We have the freedom to choose our own attitude in any given set of circumstances; we have the freedom to choose our own way. We have the power of choice. You have the power of choice. What do you choose to do now? It is my fervent hope that you will choose to combine your desire for change with your power of choice and implement your Personal Power Plan. Now. Today. Remember, your future is being determined now. Your future is being determined by the thoughts, actions, and attitudes you harbor today.

This is a good time to consider and study Reinhold Niebuhr's *"Serenity Prayer"*:

> "God, give us grace to accept with
> serenity the things that cannot be
> changed—the courage to change the
> things which should be changed—and
> the wisdom to distinguish the one
> from the other."

Remember, you have the power to choose and to change. You can choose your own attitude; you can choose your own way. You can change the things in your life that you wish to change. You do have the wisdom and the ability to do whatever it takes to accomplish your goals, realize your ambitions, and manifest your desires. Make your choices and your changes wisely. Work with, not against, the universal laws. Work with the advertising concept of repetition. Write your own life script and listen, repetitively, to your future. Remember: What you say—to yourself—is what you get. Use the power of personal programming.

Let your Personal Power Plan be your passport to the life of your dreams, to the life you deserve.

Author & Artists' Bios

Alice C. Potter [1928-2018] was a radio and television broadcaster for more than 30 years. Starting out as "Alice in Slumberland", as a late-night radio disco jockey in Plattsburgh, NY, where she firsted Howard Stern as a "Shock Bra", much to the chagrin of her daughter who was in high school at the time.

Alice quickly moved into TV as an on-camera persnality in the late 1950's when all programming was "live". Her first TV show was an afternoon cooking/guest show co-hosted with Bird Burdan—way before Julia Child. She co-hosted games shows a la Vanna White, did innumerable radio and on-camera TV commercials, was a part-time newscaster and weather girl, and hosted several daily TV talks shows in Plattsburgh and in Sioux Falls.

Eventually, Alice relocated to the Bay Area to "start all over" at KRE and KPAT—now KBLX— radio in Berkeley where she held many behind-the-scenes assignments, which lead to her becoming General Manager of two San Francisco Bay Area radio Stations and a television station. Her appointment to GM of KRE in 1974 made her the first woman station manager in the country.

After leaving KRE, Alice was a broadcast executive for the Associated Press covering Northern California and Nevada. She was an active member of the National Speakers Association and presented workshop seminars. Link to Alice's book: roninpub.com/ppp.html.

Elena Facciola is an illustrator in San Francisco Bay area and Alice's good friend.

Brian Groppe is creative director for *Memphis Magazine* and *Inside Memphis Business*. He previously served as senior design director / photo editor for Towery Publishing's Urban Tapestry Series of city photojournals. Brian is the recipient of numerous regional and national awards. He holds a BFA in graphic design from California College of the Arts.

Chris "Huneysuckle" Ellis is a contributing ellustrator for *Memphis Magazine*. He provides sophisticated doodles when stories don't have quite enough words to fill the page. A native of Memphis, Ellis now lives in Los Angeles. Chris is always ready with sketch pad in hand when Memphis bespeaks one of his Ellistrations.

RONIN
Books for Independent Minds
roninpub.com

Please visit

CPSIA information can be obtained
at www.ICGtesting.com
Printed in the USA
LVHW041709130219
607433LV00002B/228

$18.95

CREATE YOUR PERSONAL
POWER PLAN
FOR A HEALTHY, HAPPY
FULFILLING LIFE

by **Alice C. Potter**
Illustrated by **Elena Facciola**

Create Your Personal Power Plan shows how to put optimism to practical use. How to take command of your life and leave behind your fears through simple and sound steps. Shares ten simple rules that can change your life, helpful guidelines for creating personal affirmations, along with inspirational quotations, motivational stories and anecdotes demonstrating use of the commandments.

Create Your Personal Power Plan tells how the power of positive thinking promotes personal success; techniques to replace negative thoughts and actions with positive ones; how to overcome fears and anxiety, and how to transform dreams into reality.

Create Your Personal Power Plan includes strategies to create and achieve personal goals, along with stories of success, words of wisdom, and inspirational exercises to gain confidence and overcome procrastination.

ISBN 978-157951275-0

Self-Help
RONIN/Berkeley, CA
roninpub.com

51895>

9 781579 512750